K-O-R-N FILLED

ALLMYNACK

PUBLISHED BY GAGE PUBLISHING

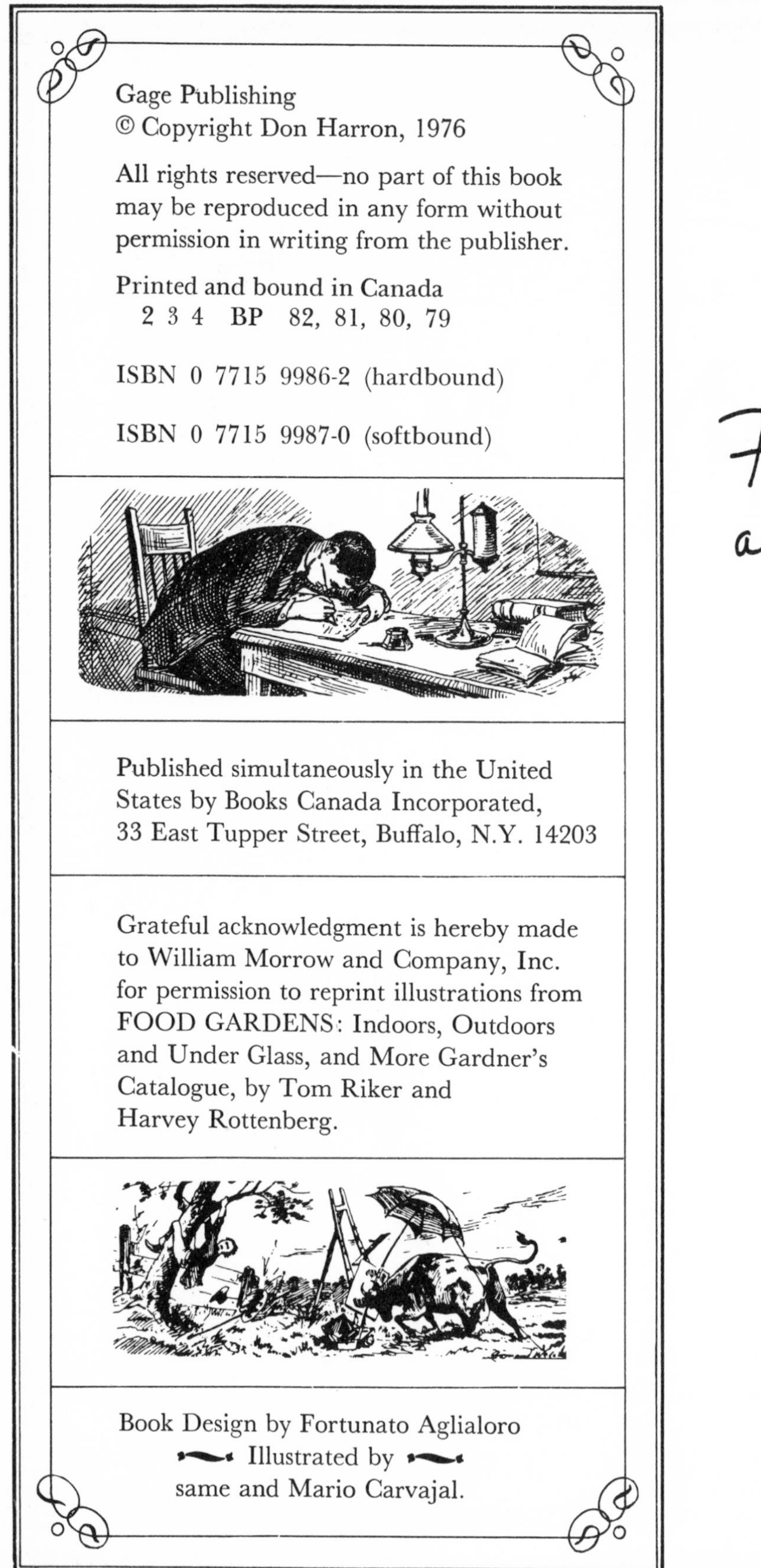

Gage Publishing

Printed and bound in Canada
2 3 4 BP 82, 81, 80, 79

ISBN 0 7715 9986-2 (hardbound)

ISBN 0 7715 9987-0 (softbound)

Published simultaneously in the United States by Books Canada Incorporated, 33 East Tupper Street, Buffalo, N.Y. 14203

Grateful acknowledgment is hereby made to William Morrow and Company, Inc. for permission to reprint illustrations from FOOD GARDENS: Indoors, Outdoors and Under Glass, and More Gardner's Catalogue, by Tom Riker and Harvey Rottenberg.

Book Design by Fortunato Aglialoro
Illustrated by
same and Mario Carvajal.

For Lionel
and Delsia

CHARLIE FARQUHARSON'S

K-O-R-N FILLED

ALLMYNACK

Published for 1 hole conzecutive yeer and writ in plane simple langwidge to be understood by the commonest people.

Containing advice fer the future and the pasture; How to live off the lien of the land; Wild life fer all the famly; Plumming fer outdoresmen (See Crappers fur Trappers); Inteerior desecrating fer the idle poor; Down t'erth hints fer yer sick nurse; Curing hams and other home entertainmints; Draining and leaching of vegibles; Skinning and stuffing of small aminals; Curing and Tanning of children; and other Misselanus Items

Incloodin
How to rid yerself of Glanders, Spavins, and Heaves with Embarkations, Essences and Elicksirs
and Bonus Tip
How to rid yer Chickens of the Pox.

PUBLISHED BY GAGE PUBLISHING

FRIEND OF THE CHILDLESS!!!!

A Absolute Musk

DOCTOR RUSE'S KIDNEY

— AND —

BLADDER DRINK

Your Non-injurious Excitant

LOVE'S ASSISTANT • PARENT OF PLEASURE
FOUNTAIN OF POWER • HOPE FOR THE AGED
PROLONGER OF YOUTH • PRESERVES THE HONOR OF THE FAMILY

Compounded of Indian Hemp, Oil of Cantharides, (Spanish Flies) Arsenick, Fossforus, and Stricknine

A NERVEEN STIMULANT AND RENOVATOR

Used to the Last by the Late Sultan of Turkey.

**slightly bitter to the taste* (Surgin' Genral's Report)

Calendar Ruling Yer Periods

FOR

THE TWELVE SIGNS OF THE ZODIAC
AND THEIR BAWDY RELATIONS

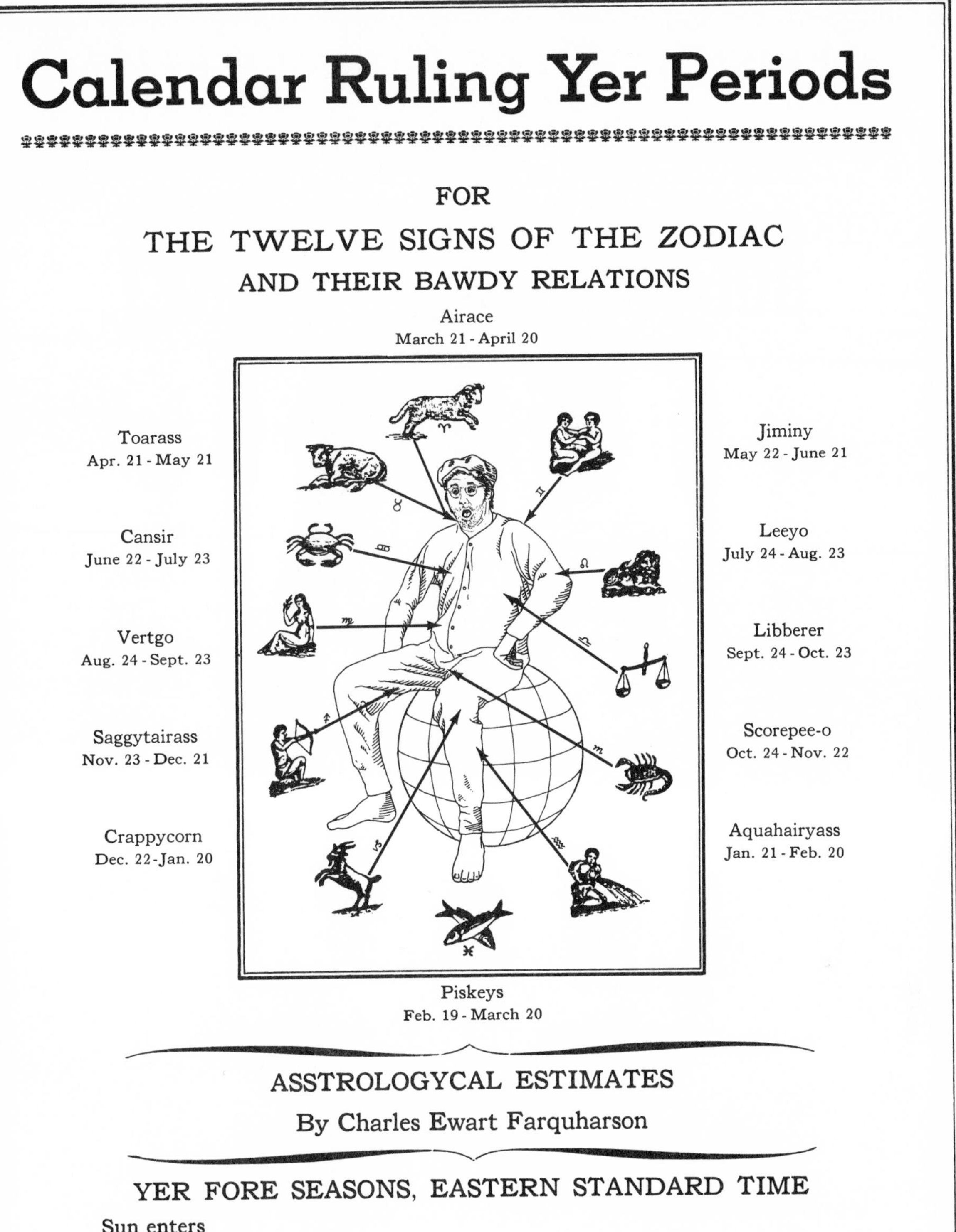

ASSTROLOGYCAL ESTIMATES

By Charles Ewart Farquharson

YER FORE SEASONS, EASTERN STANDARD TIME

Sun enters Sign	Long.	Const'n	
♑	270°	♐	and Winter begins, Dec. 22, A.M.
♈	0°	♓	and Spring begins, Mar. 20, A.M.
♋	90°	♊	and Summer begins, June 21, A.M.
♎	180°	♍	and Autumn begins, Sept. 22, P.M.

ARE YOU DRIVING THE BRAIN

At The Expense of the Body?

Suffering from loss of Strength, Flesh and Nerve ? ?

Repair all three with

Hipwell's Compound

of

Beef Iron and Wine

Builds your nerve as it tears your flesh, and irons everything out in the end.

Get even today ?!

Hipwell's Natural Dark Fluids McKeesters Rapids, Wis.

YER HISTERICAL ORGE-IN OF YER ASSTROLOGY

Back when yer cave-in man was yer forest's prime eevil, there warn't much to do nites eggsept rub things together and hope fer a bit of sparkin'. Ther sure warn't no TV. The only show our primitiv incesters had was up in the sky –yer Milky Way Hour brot to you by yer lokel Galexlaxy, and feechering yer Big Dippy and Spiro's Nebulous–not what you'd call a prime time mover.

Mind you once in a wile things britened up: lightening or mebbe even a totalled E-clips. And them as watched long enuff begun to notiss them little flickers on yer hevvinly screen goin thru the changes–slower'n molasses–jist like yer avrage Sope Opry–but snailing acrost the sky so's you'd mind it. And sum of them little blinkers moved faster'n others–these was yer planits, and then there was yer flashers in the pan, yer meatier-rites and yer little haff-assteroids. And fer a treet, ever so often, a cumit, a sorta roamin' candle with a lotta spark to its tale.

Now yer Pree-histeric Man, what else had he got to look up to? That's why these twitchy hevvinly bawdies becum his gods. Yer sun and yer moon nacherly, they was first. But jist to cover all bases, our Missing Lynks figgered out names fer them little lightnin-buggers that kept wandrin' offa yer beetin track. Nuthin' was left to chants. Everything good er bad was dun to you by sum Dee-uh-titty, fer god's sake.

It was yer Baby-loany-uns first kep track of all these constellarpations movemints. They writ them down on tables (had no paper I gess). They jist wanted to know that the Universal was folding up as it should.

Yer Drudes in England unhinged some big stones and heaved them more'n a hundert mile down to Stonehinged. It's a mistry to this day how they got ther rocks off, but you kin still perdict yer Sun's eclips from ther erections.

Them Peeramid clubs hard by Ejypt dun the same thing. Yer Faro weeler-deelers had lotsa slaves fer to do it, and at first histerians thot they was jist bilding a funeral parler fer to house ther own sarcoffyguss. Turns out these here Eternal Tryangles was lined up with Pole-arse yer North Star, and it more or less told yer Ejippt fellah wen the Nile wud let him bend over and have a good crop. (Some famuss Faros was Ramsey yer First, and Ptallme . . . the "p" is silent, as in swimming.)

Even yer South Amurrican Asstex up yer Andy Mountings, they tuk a lotta steps up to git a good vue of yer Horrorscope screen in the sky. It was quite a star trek up there too. You kin still see ther tempels at Popo-cot-a-piddle and Chicken Itzy, both below-yer-belt boarder towns.

Back over to yer Grease, they was too bizzy fillossofizin fer to git much into yer Sodyack, but even that big Geek Plate-o was told all about it by his teecher, Arsetoddle.

Yer Roamins, they was more give over to Oggery . . . wich is splittin pidgins and lookin at ther end-tails. But the empurer Juvenile, he brung back the fad of seeing stars. But they had to drop the pidgins cuz they got in the way of sky-watching.

With the fall-out of yer Romin Umpire yer Assterology declined. Mind you, even the Three Wise Fellas that bring the gold and murr and franken-stines got there by star gazing.

And Julius Seizure give a big goose to the hole bizness wen he cum up with that calender had twelve parts to it, and called all them peeriods munthlies.

Up till then one man's Chewsdy had bin another man's Thirsdy. But it's yer farmer that needs a time table more'n anybuddy, becuz if a farmer ain't in seeson he don't make it. He has to be gittin' in the hay in Jooly, and thrashin' about in August . . . everything has to be dun weekly at the rite time.

So here's the hole rundown munth by munth, showin' wher yer Asster-logical sines fits into the parts of yer body.

PLANITS OF YER UNIVERSAL

YER SUN: Senter of the hole rang-dang-doo, and alwaze in heet. Also suffers from comiscal blackheads wich gives us a lot of statick. Yer Sun is God of yer hart and spine as far as it goes.

YER MOON: Goddess of brests and bawdy flooids. It travills round yer Erth in a lippstickle orbit, and is uninhibited except fer what yer assternuts left after ther last nockturnally mission.

MURKRY: God of X Communications . . . (Adult only) . . . Also God of fish ever since yer nukuler fell-out. Cops used to stop me if I had my Murkry fulla fish. Now that my fish is fulla murkry they don't seem to care. Murkry is yer smallist and most hothouse of yer planits. They say it has no atmusfeer. But boy, kin it put peeple under the infloonce. Speshully Virgins and Twins.

VEENIS: Godass of bewdy and the lumber reegions. As a planit, not so much in heet as you'd think. More like smog. But as the brite lite in our lokel fermamint, when she comes out in her erly edition in yer twilite zone, she gits a rise out of a lot of us, speshully yer Libbers and Toarasses.

MARSE: There are no canals in Veenis, I don't care what yer travel books say. But them Marse bars looks the alimentary kind. It's rite Marse shud be behind bars on accounta he's the God of violents, and wirld whores. Controls yer Airaces.

JOOPTER: Yer biggest planit and a bit of a gas. Rools over Saggytairass like a king. On a tellyscope all you can see is yer Big Bands. I heer ther comin back.

SLATTERN: Pritty fur-out, but kin rotate rings round the rest of them. Close-up looks like a preggrunt frizzbee. To be slatternine is to be crool and distempered. Hangs over Crappycorns.

YERANUS: Hung well-back in yer Galexlaxy, and keeps its mean distants from the rest of them. God of preeversion and sexual D.V. Asian.

NEPCHEWN: Exerts big pull on Yeranus and makes water and gas at will.

PLUTOE: God of big bizness, and a dog of a star, it leans toward other planits if unleashd. In charge of vulcanoes, erthquakes, and ScoreP.o.s.

YER BIRTHDAY FORTCHUNE AND GUIDE

If you were ever born
DECEMBER 22 up til JANYERRY 20
Yer astrological sine is CRAPPYCORN
Yer ruling planit is SLATTERN

THE YEAR AHEAD FOR ALL CRAPPYCORNERS: He who hesitates, has lots. Watch fer fowl-ups, and keep a firm hand on yer resorces. Coast the first haff, then recycle yer Karmic sluggishness with a good dose of Murkry entwined with Joopiter. Let yerself go in yer last third. This can be confusing but with a frootful climax. One thing more. Get a second opinion.

CRAPPYCORNERS is one of yer erthy tipes, with clove hoofs and horny, too, if yer simbol-minded.

Seems they was born to git other peeple's goats, and tend to butt in and paw the turf till ther nanny comes. They are Saturnday's childern, a cold dry planit in yer soler sistern on accounta she's yer most distant, which garntees all you kids a swell time if you kin wait till yer old-aged.

LUCKY DAY: Natcherly Saturnday, but most goatish peeple have to wait till Saturnday nite to git lucky.

LUCKY CULLERS: Yer only good one is purpul. Them others is gray, green, black and brown. I spose you cud always go to one of yer Holloween balls drest as a ded tree.

LUCKY FLOWRS: Flacks, poppy and holly. That means you kin wear linnins and smoke opeyum at Chrissmus.

LUCKY JIMSTONES: Garnit, sapfire, amafist, onicks and moon-stoned. Best of all tho is yer Load stone (Oxhide of arn). This is not too desecrative as joolery but can be a powerful maggot fer to attrack the opposit of yer sex. Ware round yer neck in a jockular vane, and suck prospecks in under that holley–then yer set fer a big nite of roamants.

FAVRIT PLACES: Seeclooded.

SEX DRIVE: Crappycorners is late bloomers, coshus at first, but extra good in the long hall. Practickle too, like they want to know frum the back of the car does the place have a dubble bed and a stalled shower. Anmal husbandry note. Gotes is fond of yernating at each other.

WEAK POINTS: Keep away from neebones and simler joints.

FAVRIT DECEASES: Roomtism, chillz, and ex-enema.

VOCATIONAL GUIDENCE: Be a hostler, sheppurd, or sibble servent. You make good diplamattresses, scavengers, and sweepers (tho Crappercorn broom-men is genrully a little weak around the lamposts). Also robbers.

BIG NAME CRAPPYCORNS: Josiph Stallion, (yer Serviet premiere that was) and Queen Lizbeth 11. (wat happened to the other nine?)

LOOKS: Besides clove hoofs and chin-hare, Crappycorners are of meejum hite, boney, longnosed, with narrer chins, skinny necks, and dark thin public hair and eyes. These are permamint feechers so don't argew.

GOOD TRATES: Spare in ther speech, and prudint, but allus knows where the action is. They sure git the goods outa life. In the old days they was cunning in the curing of lether, which makes them now stricter pairints than most, as they still tan a lot of hides. And that's only the good parts.

OFFAL TRATES: Mean and meloncollie. If ther stars is outa ther orbits, look out. This here goatish bunch sins willyfully and nilly. They becum great flesh eeters and end up with bad breth. Quarlsum as a cut cat, fretful as a cope-in saw, jellus, stubbern, and secretif. Wisht ya'd never bin born? Too late.

HELTH HINTS: Bein a goat, you all got stomicks of arn, kin eet anything, and probly have. But nobuddy's yit seen a stuft goat, or a drunk goat, and ya'd have to go a pritty mile fer to find even a ded goat. Crappycorns is notoaryus long livers and wen the rest of us is gone or burried, these here scavavengers will still be around, cleenin up.

Fishin thru the Ice for yer Maraschino Cherry.

JANYERRY

CHARLIE'S DALY DIAREE

Jan. 1: Beginnin of a new Anal Domino. Cums the Rezzlution.

Jan. 2: Goes yer Rezzlution. Try Hare of yer Dog.

Jan. 3: Son rises at 9:30 A.M. Sets around the house all day.

Jan. 4: New Moon. (Re-run on Chanel Number Five with half Jinett Macdonalds and half Nelson Eddy).

Jan. 5: Superbowl. (Plugged up again.)

Jan. 6: Time fer a short walk in the woods. Better still—install new skeptic tank.

Jan. 7: Time to re-sickle yer Chrismus tree. Heave it in lake by dragging on ice, then Law of Gravelty will do her by spring. Makes a good crappie bed fer them fish.

Jan. 8: Dark. Clearing tords morning.

Jan. 9: Blustery conditions upstairs. Large mass undisturbed. Son refuzes to rise, is thrust from warm bed onto cold bysickle seat.

Jan. 10: Jersey cow fresh agin.

Jan. 11: Herfurd bull even fresher. Gets face slapt with Jersey tale.

Jan. 12: Rooster crows 2 A.M.

Jan. 13: Speshul dinner fer retiring rooster. Tuff.

Jan. 14: Gale. Storm. She has the re-runs on Chanel No. 5.

Jan. 15: Fair spell. Wife complanes of dizzyness and a hot flash.

Jan. 16: Son sets 2:15 A.M. and is roze up agin at 6:50 A.M. Big chore.

Jan. 17: Intermitten showers, plus a bath fer the wife.

Jan. 18: Time to remove stumps. Make appt. with dentist.

Jan. 19: Salt lick time. Put blocks to cows.

Jan. 20: Check wife's cold frame. Get her to warm her feet fore comin to bed.

Jan. 21: Clean chickenhouse. Keep mouth shut.
Jan. 22: Fallow field. Get my rocks off.
Jan. 23: Make whey fer the hogs. Also selected shorts.
Jan. 24: Clip stubble. Go to church.
Jan. 25: Buy coal? Oil? Yer burning question.
Jan. 26: Son spots. My boy Orville tends his hives.
Jan. 27: Bad storm. Gang, gang, the hail's all here.
Jan. 28: Hand grease Alice Chalmers.
Jan. 29: Pop corn around fire. Put on Bloojay plaster.
Jan. 30: Snow. Son tries to rite his name. Gits halfway.
Jan. 31: Fishing thru the ice. Sure love them marriano cherries.

THOT FER THIS MUNTH

One good turn will git you mor'n haff the quilts.

BE A DIPPER!

Let us start you in this elegant business.

Snuff yourself to riches, by putting your business into other people's noses.

BENNY THE DIP,
Pick Hotel, Spray Acres, Virginia.

ASSAY fer JANYERRY

(by Charles Ewart Farquharson in season)

This is the munth wen the ground is hardern a postman's sock, and them roads slippyer than a fancy woman's heel. Childern goes to school in yer Dark Ages, and comes home in yer twy-lit zone that makes them think they is working yer gravyard shift.

It makes ya beleeve them Meatier-ollygists when they say yer Iced Aged is comin back fer the re-runs of that ten thousand yeer cold snap they give us a millenema ago. The thermalstat got turned down so far it extinkted all them Dinashores and Brontysoreasses. And wen them big glassy-ears slid down from yer friggid North everything got froze but wages and prices. Amerka becum pritty well uninhibted.

Later, acorse, it warmed up, only thing stayed hardend was yer Articks, and the rest of Amerka becum one big melting plot. But they say the dee-frosting is jist about over and we'll be startin' to seize up in our erogenous zones agin. Let's face it, we've had the hots.

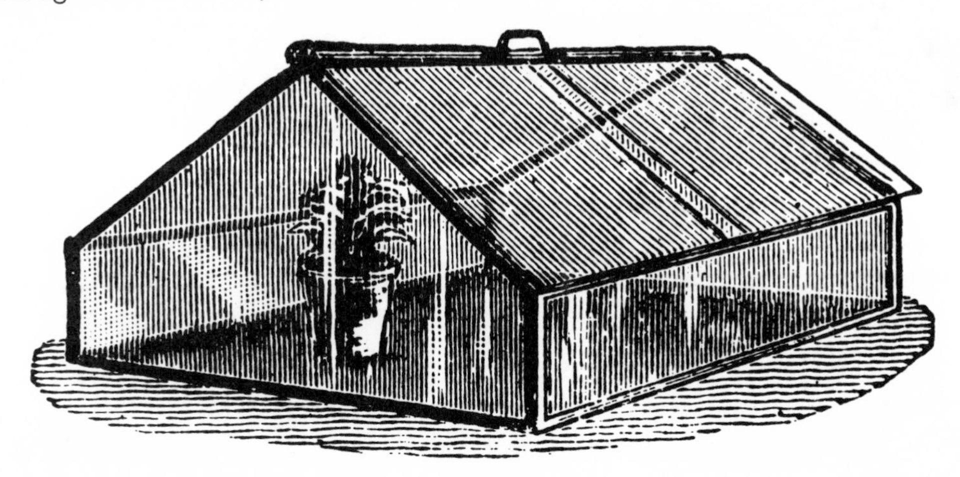

HELPFUL HINTS ABOUT GITTIN THRU THIS MUNTH:

Don't take yer cold frame into the garden as yet. It's a good time to think about fertlizing tho. Locate a good sorce of manoor. Try looking dreckly under a cow. This Back to the Land movemint is called Orgasmic Gardning. It's the real thing, and garntees when it comes to city peeples in the summer, you will have one of the best spreds around. But fer now, keep yer feet in the stove, practiss tying yer own flies and wait to git sprung by spring.

THE CURING AND TANNING OF KIDS

A small stock investmint . . . getting yer famly's goat.

Since Wimmen's Librium come in, the goat has replaced the wife as the poor man's cow. More peeple in the wirld drinks goats' milk than cow's. This makes yer goats the reel foster muthers of mankine.

Goats are herd animals, and not obcene, despite ther pubic relations. There are many miscontraceptions about goats–how like ther all inhibited by the Devvil, and never stop gettin' horny.

See fer yerself. Go to a Spring Showing of goats and settle fer nuthin but the best. Come away with a hansom topgoat of yer own. But don't nanny er billy them. Goats is called bucks and does. Bucks is the one with scent glands under ther nobs. That's wher the story comes in that they are nature's wethervains n' you kin always tell wich way the wind is blowin with one of them around. This is not true from Febuary to August wen goats kin hardly breed.

But look out from October to Janyerry, wen the flirtin starts. To attrack the doe, yer buck will urnate on his beard. (Now you have to be suple to do that!) This turns peeple off but does on. As soon as yer buck gits a small deposit on the wattles, he is like Cathern DeNerve on Channel 5. Durin this time any doe will do it fer a buck.

Listen, that's how kids get born. Never mind them stories about the birds, the bees and the drugstore. And that's when yer doe perduices more milk than yer cow per square udder, even tho they is outnumbered in the teet department 4 to 2. But cows are lucky to get half as many caffs, becuz goats pervide multipple births.

Kidding aside, goats milk is good fer yumans too. It don't cream itself at the top, but is otherwise normil. And it don't depend on yer bag size. Like with us, large teats kin turn out to be all that meat and no gravy. Besides a well-stacked goat is hung so low you'd have to milk her with a pie-plate.

Don't keep the kids too long before weening them. With all them kids around it meens congested udders at rush hour. Take them off the mothers and pop them on the bottle.

Funny thing, kids that don't git weened off soon, and stick to ther mothers, grow up wilder than yer bottled babies. Now Doctor Spock don't agree with that. Spock, he's that peedyassed-trishun with the pointy ears has the re-runs on yer TV Star Drek. He bleeves in kids that suck around ther mothers. And he don't bleeve in tannin ther hides, not ever. I gess wen he was small and bad, his mother used to pin his ears back and hang him on the line to cry.

And he's still got this hang-up. What he calls yer udder frusteration.

Anuther thing Spock woodn't agree with–most boy kids is caster-rated by the time ther eight weeks old. But, except fer the odd stud, yer kid has to be renderd interfectual or he'll insest on doin it with his kid sister as erly as three munths.

Now Doc Spock brung up a hole generation of you, and never delt with none of this. All of you untanned and uncured . . . that's why yer all goin to massedge parlers with toplist massuses. If you'd bin brung up on a farm and had to strip fourteen topless Holesteen twice a day you woodn't have to subblemate yerself with some mass-hoor in a belly-rub parler rubbing you the rong way, and spankin off yer guilt edges.

No wonder them stockbrokers are walkin' the Wall Streets chewin' on a big fat seegar. And no wonder they want to be serve by topless waitrusses wen they git that inedible creme substitute put in ther coffee, and can't git at the reel thing.

Go ahed–Git yer goat. Why let the guvmint do it for you?

MUSKEENEE TABLOID TEA.

presents a new departure . . .

For Salt rheum, scald head, and Scrofulating Pimples.

Also a Tricopherous for the Hair, which removes external ailments of the head, preventing grayness, thinning, scurvy, and allowing it to be moist, thick and lustrous on top.

MUSKEENEE Common Stock Company Youngstown, Ohio.

YER BIRTHDAY FORTCHUNE AND GUIDE

If you were ever born
JANYERRY 21 up til FEBYAIRY 20
Yer astrological sine is AQUAHAIRYASS
Yer ruling planit is YERANUS

THE YEAR AHEAD FOR ALL AQUAHAIRYASSES: You have jist spent a year under Yeranus, so don't overlode yer wiring. Plug out of the power struggle fer a bit. After Febyairy, Marse moves out of the house and Venis makes arrangements to move in. This allows you to take the bully by the horns and spred yerself a bit. Dare everything. Go shopping. By the end of the yeer much credit will return to you. (But be sure to choose another card.)

AQUAHAIRYASS is yer common carrier of water, and one of yer fixed ones. This is sposed to be the donning of yer Age of Aquahairyass, like it was sung in that rotten-roll open-Hair show with all them Hippie-Optimists standing there singin full frontle fer sevral pubic feet.

But that figgers, because the simble fer this sine is making waves, so you can expeck a lotta rebbles and excentricks. Also inventers. Aquahairyass is yer mother of inventers, so fergit the old saying about incessity being yer mother's invention.

FISCAL FEECHERS: Reglar, almost hansom, in a store-dummy sorta way. Not exactly sissy, but more town-boy than tom-boy, leanin' to yer trans-vestry-ite.

STRENGTHS: Pergressively friendly, interested in yer Brothers Hood of Man, but semmy-detached, conserned for youmanity in the abstrack. Tend to foller conventions, like a second cuzzin of mine went all the way with a Shriner to Toronto.

WEAKNESSES: Fibb a lot, and like to be manipple-aters.

LUCKY BERTHSTONE: Sap-hire or amafist.

LUCKY FLOWR: Yer pansy or yer daffydill.

LUCKY CULLERS: Lavendoor, other past-tell shades.

LUCKY NUMBER: 7. (Yer combinations of 4 and 3, 5 and 2, 6 and 1, also makes yer point.)

FAVRIT READING: Sucksess storys. (This is impractickle, to wich you are inclined. Insted of reading about someone elt'ses happy end, you shud git up offa yer own.)

FAVRIT PLACE: Where the action is.

LUCKY DAY: Saturdays. So wait fer yer weak end.

SEX SINE: You are Airy, so git hot with Fire sines like Airace or Saggyterrace. Stay away from Toarass or Scorepee-o. Aquahairyass is under Yeranus and likes love, but likes, too, to be changed reglar. Divorce is more poplar than holey macarony. Lots of prospecks fer yer Unhook-of-the-Month Club. Yer inventory nature means you'll probly end up a big wife-swopper. Also tend to sctional preversion with other D.V.8's.

PAIRINT AND CHILD: Aquahairyans are modren, and commyune together a lot, and enrole kids in neerst MontySorry boreding school.

HELTH: Even tho you know all the ankles, keep them rapt in cold wethers, and watchout fer veryclose vanes, and hardning of yer archerys.

BIG NAMES: James Dean (not yer TV sossidge but yer Rebble without Caws). Tomass Edson, he made yer bulbs incan-decent. WolfGang Moe Zart, who kept track of all his movements and writ them down into sympathies to be playd by classified orkesters. Jim E. Duranty, the winner by a nose.

Yer Cock and Pullet.

FEBYAIRY

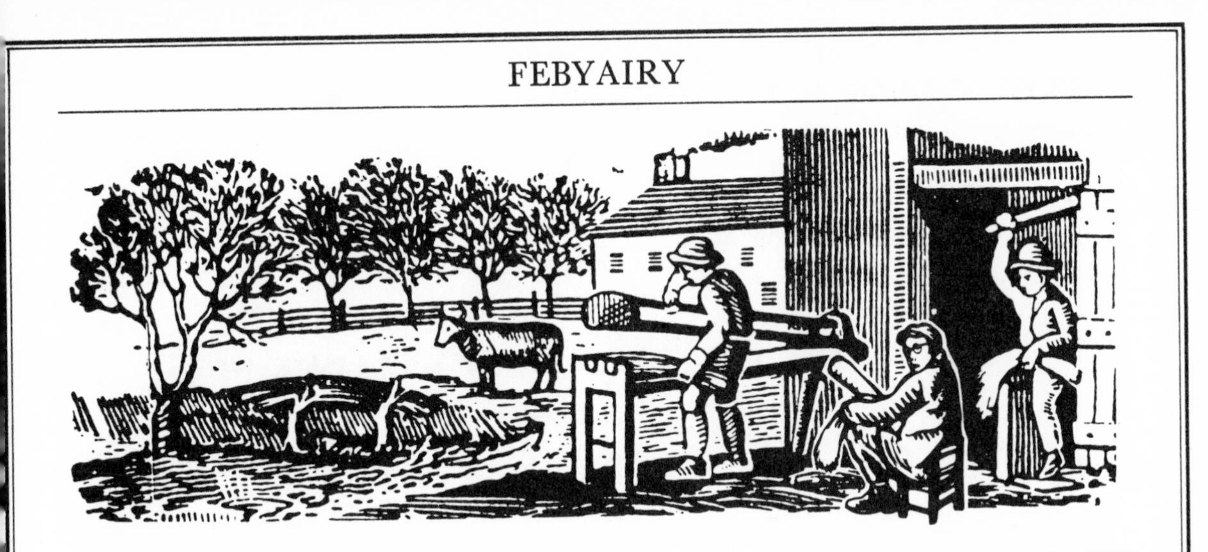

CHARLIE'S DALY DIAREE

Feb. 1: Ground Hawg Day. The Shadder knows.
Feb. 2: Pancake Chewsday. Better fatten up fer Lent.
Feb. 3: Ashes Wensdy. Also papers and garbidge.
Feb. 4: Wether goes thru changes.
Feb. 5: Intermitten slow and sleet.
Feb. 6: Wife sez to put my hand in front of my face wen I sneeze to catch my teeth.
Feb. 7: Time to cut the corn agin.
Feb. 8: Had to put a Blewjay plaster on corn.
Feb. 9: Mild spell. Tried to start something in wife's hot bed.
Feb. 10: Time to re-charge batterys. Positive of this, doo to negative termnal response.
Feb. 11: Time off. Nothing to do but widdle.
Feb. 12: Local option lection. Vote as you lick.
Feb. 13: Up the poll agin. How dry we am. Next time vote as I lick, but vote offen.
Feb. 14: Vallantine's Day. Fergot card fer wife and former sweetart.
Feb. 15: Vallantine's Day Massacker. Went out and bot card.
Feb. 16: Late starter with chicks. Remember to put bran in ther shorts.
Feb. 17: Son wants to start with chicks. Put salt-peter in his bran.
Feb. 18: Ring round moon. Time to cleen bathtub.
Feb. 19: Son spots. Early spring brake-out. The acne of perfection.
Feb. 20: Water trubble. Wife gits a run in her hydrolick pump hose.
Feb. 21: Buy haff ton pig starter. (Thou. swill)
Feb. 22: Full moon. Watch fur hair on shoulders of son'n heir.
Feb. 23: Straiten male box. Son missed his turn in our car.

Feb. 24: Foul supper. Lunch was a bit better.
Feb. 25: Cold enuff to freeze the knots off a pine.
Feb. 26: Staid home. Put feet in stove. Later roasted nuts.
Feb. 27: The big question. Contack C or goosegrease in flanellette?
Feb. 28: Scool consert. Son pulls his first drape.

THOT FER THIS MUNTH

It's a good thing this here wasn't a Leap Year or a lotta stockbrokers mite of taken it.

GETTIN' MULCH?

Trash as a Way of Life, and other Rotten Matters.

Until you till, there's a lot can be done by letting yerself be waste deep in mulch. Mulch is jist another way of sayin fertlizer. (There are other ways too humerus to menshun.) It is also wat they call in yer better-bred circles, artifishul insulation.

Nature herself is yer biggest mulcher. She drops her leeves offa her trees, then does a big cover-up with a blankit of snow. This allows everything underneeth to bed down and take its natcheral inner corse. Fer a garden shood not be left naked fer to expose itself all winter. Keep yer cold out and yer warm parts in, with holes fer to breethe, purty much like that Norweegy undyware.

Mulch is nature's own original de-composition, and in the end we are all de-composers. Mulch is jist offal recyclin itself . . . its own persnal back-to-the-land movemint. A gardner can ern a living by bringing back the ded and pilin it on – coffee grounds, tea bags, banana peels, apple cores, egg shells, ded flowrs, korn kobs, bubble-gum rappers, leef mold, marsh grass, woodchips, sawdust, spoiled hay – the hole rang-dang-doo wich sitty peeples calls garbidge is something that makes dirt rich, yet it remanes dirt cheep. You'll be sprised how soon the rot sets in. Remember to pack a mulch before you go off fer the day.

How can mulch be made attracktive short of gift-rapping yer garbidge? Well, if you insist on bein a exteerior deckerator, put yer mulch in the blender, add water, mebbe use a little side dressin, oil er vineger, then chop, chop – top-dress before dinner and have yer mulch agin jist afore bed-time. Otherwise, if you wanna be ornamental in yer own garden, I suggest you get a good sunburn down in Florrider, come back, stand on one laig, bare as a bird on yer front lawn, and peeple will think you are a pink flamingo.

Some peeple are agin mulchers in any way. That's what I heer from the gripe vine, but you can allus expeck pro and con artists in every garden. If you and the wife disagrees about mulch, here's what to do. During Lent, divide yer bed into two parts (haff-way thru the spring) and you kin mulch in yer haff of the bed without disturbin yer bitter haff.

Remember with the price of fud the way it is, Victry Gardens is coming back into stile. We'll soon be a nation of Happy Hoers.

If you remove yer mulch, do it on a cloudy day, so that yer yung shoot-outs don't git blasted by the sun's ultry-violents. A plant don't need all that much sunshine, compaired to rain. Look at yer nuts in them tropical rain forsts. But once in a wile you gotta open yer plants and let some air in.

Here's some hints. Don't bother mulching yer radishes, becuz they repeet themselves anyway. But keep that rotten vegible matter round the rest of yer plants' bottoms. Fer what's goin' on down there is the faint stirrin be-neeth yer feet of tiny micro-orgasms. Jist leave them creepy little crawlies to ther work. Remember, you can't hit the jackpot without a slug er two in it. Snails can be useful as ex-cargo and sold to Frenchmen. But avoid fungus. It may be necessary to fung off every once in a wile. My wife finds Pete Moss very absorbing in a hot bed, fer controlling yer erosenous zones.

If you must use chemmicle herbysides, nite rates are cheeper. Don't git yer root in a knot from cut-worm, Mexcan Beatles and yer non-praying, non-compost mantis. But watch the chemmicles; try not to catch ammonia. Catch dew insted. Fer this you need a nert mulch – the kind that jist lies there – and does nothin but absorb everythin goin' on – like a old married woman long over-dew. Fer this kind of mulch, cover the issue with tissue, old boards, tarpaper, alumnus foil, or even Polly Eveleen. This keeps yer soil fryable without burnin yer plants off. Scuff with a hoe, or even yer shoe.

So don't let life go down the drain. Make yer garden yer compost pile. Or if you're too lazy – the vice of that versa. You'll be amazed how eesy it is to ferment in heet.

HOW TO BE IN HEET ALL WINTER

Here's a hot flash fer all you seenyer sittizens. You can beet yer own energy crisis without puttin on a swetter, turnin the lites out, and going to bed every nite at sundown. That kinda thing only leeds to yer copulation explosion.

It's better to stay up, keep yer pores open, and burn off nature's energy what's standing up by itself in the forst. Fer yer tree is a renewable resorce. Unlike us, it goes to seed only to rize agin.

Never mind yer oil burner. Let go yer natcheral gas. Go back to shovin yer log into a cast-arn stove. If yer a pree-flab owner, jist cut a hole in the roof and shove yer flu up. But be sure to stuff up yer space around it with the assbestest insulation you can find. And make sure you and yer wife are well-stacked. If you both take karatty lessens you can split the kindling between you.

Here's a questin a lotta peeple ask. What makes them loud pops when yer log is on the fire? Well, that's jist forst air, same as you and me when we eat too fast.

What shood you burn? Well, hickry and oak is best, but hard maple wen you git down to it will give a good peece of ash. Remember with wood, the more dense you are the longer yer slow burn. All you need fer to be a cut-up is a ax, a maul and a crost-cut saw. Mebbe a sludge-hammer if the wife don't feel like it. That's what wood-craft is all about. Bein crafty in gittin somebuddy else to cut the wood.

YER BIRTHDAY FORTCHUNE AND GUIDE

If you were ever born
FEBYAIRY 21 up til MARCH 20
Yer astrological sine is PISKEYS
Yer ruling planit is NEPCHEWN

THE YEAR AHEAD FOR ALL PISKEENS: Think before you swim. Try some of that transcontinental mediation. It will git you out of the unstable. The new moon coming over the sextile may leave romantic matter on yer collar, but avoid too rabid a transit frum yer accustomed square. Never mind yer second house until you clear yer passage from the first. When in doubt, chaste yer blues away.

PISKEYS is yer Fishy foke (not to be cornfused with them Leprus Cons from IreLand, yer faery fokes). Yer Piskeys sine is a pair of fishies on a leesh, the one swimmin' one way, and th'other swimmin' the t'other–yer upper and yer down-streemer, showin' that there's some Piskeys don't know wich end is up. (Accordin to yer Sturgin-General this makes fer a shortage of cavyar aigs.)

Piskeys is rooled by yer two planits of Jupeter and Nepchewn wich makes it both yer gentlest and vilentest sine at the same time. This pairaducks is explaned by Piskeys wantin' to swim agin the current, and sometimes even bi-furk itself. This makes them yer wet dreemers of yer Sodyack. They are like the sea they swim in: offen salty, fulla hidden depfs, sudden storms, kinda weedy, and always runnin' away like yer Tide, wich acts as a detergent to them. That is why they freakwent low dives, git high, and end up on the rocks. (When they git tanked up they will do anything fer a fin.) They are always looking' fer somebuddy else to change ther water.

POSTIVE ASSPEXX: Humilititty, come-passion and simpathee.

YER NEGGATIVS: Weak, vaig, impractickle, unpunkchill.

FISCAL FEECHERS: Kinda wet. Big eyes, ovul face, full cheeks, mouth round and they genrully go thru life with it open. Lotsa foot trubble, toes tending to web . . . offen hid by Erth shoes. Not many Athleets Feat(except between the toes). Piskeys make poor road runners or street walkers.

HELTH AND DYET: Piskeys shud eat raisins, figs and proons fer to soak up sun. Them as prone to proons shooden stray too far from home. Weak chests? Try faltzies or sillycones.

SEX LIFE: Pisskeens are sloe to take the bait, and can git pritty sticky even underwater. They immerse therselves in ther love ones and jist lie there like a clam. (Except that clams shut up once in a while.) Be more aggressive and lern verse-tilty; remember yer sex act yewsually involves two persons. (altho it can go as low as one, or as high as yer Sit-down Orjy fer 500. Fer ferther details see that old Gibbon's Deecline and Fall-out frum yer Roamin' Umpire.)

MARRIDGE AND THE FAMILY: Yer Piskeys may be queer fish, but ther not loaners. They likes to swarm in cumpny. You kin go out with them fiery Saggytairasses but it'll probly be a damp squib. And yer airy Jiminy will leave you a gasper on the beech. Stick with yer Toarass and yer Crappycorn, stolid erthy sines–with eether one of them yer watery Piskey can make beautiful mud together.

PAIRINTS AND OFFSPRING: Piskeen pairints spoil ther brood somethin' terrible. So be careful you Pisky mothers, ther's nothin' worse than spoilt fish aigs.

LUCKY BERTHSTONE: Awkwa-murine.

LUCKY CULLERS: Anything fishy . . . graze, greens, mebbe lavender. Show yerself off in long flowing stuff, put lotsa shiff-on, mebbe one of them Hostess gowns, fer the sake of yer Cupcakes. Piskey men (who are not trasvestry-ites) kin jist lay in the bathtub and smile.

LUCKY FLOWRS: Loadus flowrs, but also keep lotsa water lillys in yer pad.

READING: Mistry story. Underground magzeens if they go deep enuff.

HOBBY: Numos-maticks. (Who isn't intrested in coinin munny?)

LUCKY DAY: Thursdy. (And all that it endtails.)

LUCKY NUMBER: 9. (Or 6 if yer fasing the other way.)

SONGS: Lully-byes. (Fer to put you asleep wile yer in deep.)

BEST PLACES: Water. Form yer own car pool.

BIG NAME PISKEYS: Show-pan (yer Pole Peenist who is now deecomposed.) Alber Tinestine(formerly with yer Fourth Dimention). Liz Tailer (gone fer a Burton more than once). Bobby Orr (was on the defensive fer yer Boston Brunes hocky teem, now with yer Chicago Blacocks. Bobby is a home-town boy of ours, won yer Lady Bang trophy, and had a baby soon after. Ackshully his wife had it, but Bobby got the assist.)

KAREERS: Yer Piskey shud not go in fer yer athleat's feats. They shud settle into been eether fish-mungers, nuns or alky-hollicks.

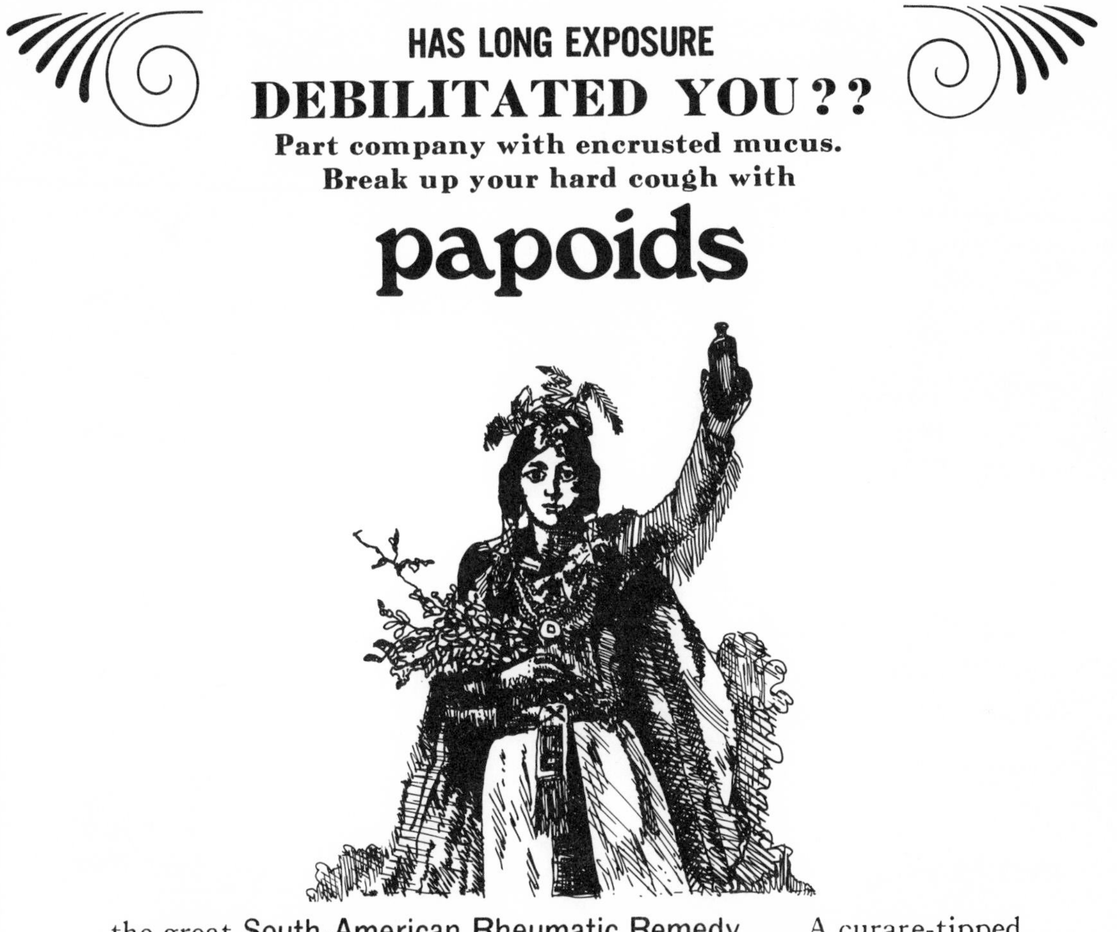

the great South-American Rheumatic Remedy . . . A curare-tipped wonder drug from the rain-washed forests of Patagonia.

Get the PAPOIDS habit. Fight inflammation now.

"I have taken and been taken with PAPOIDS for some summers, man and chief."
— A WASHINGTON SENECA.

"It frequently recovers them as seem dead."
— AN UNDERTAKER WHO WISHES TO REMAIN.

PAPOIDSCO Megantic, Maine.

Sprained your Joints?

Allcock's Porous Plaster ensures effective hardening without asphyxiation of the pores of any of your members. High perfection secured after years of diaphonous experiment.

Has America gone soft?

NEVER!

Our reputation will stand

ALLCOCK'S SOUTHRN CO.
Wilkes Barr, Penna.

UNSIGHTLY HAIR REMOVED

from the Palm of the Hand

Begone the down-cast countenance . . .
Look everyone firmly in the face!
All consultations conducted in closet.
Free eye test on request.

☞ The House of Onan ☜
Sulfa Springs, Ark.

MARCH

CHARLIE'S DALY DIAREE

March 1: Well, it come in like yer Lion's Club. Can't wate fer it to take it on the lamm.

March 2: More wind. One of our chickens with her back to it laid the same aig six times.

March 3: Lent Party at Church. Wife sang and I was page turner. Had about as much fun as a cold pancake.

March 4: Fer Lent we gotta cut down on rich fuds er we can't pay the butcher bill.

March 5: Son finds it hard to shine, much less rize before 8 A.M. He feels he was borne to be a nooner.

March 6: Wife has lenthened her skirts fer Lent.

March 7: I was told to mind my P's and Q's. Have sent away by hand-ritin' to git anal-ized.

March 8: School hollyday. True to his word, son gits up at the crack of noon.

March 9: My milkin hands swole up. Couldn't pull a thing in the barn.

March 10: Son down with spring feever. Can't work due to state of per-petchal emotion.

March 11: Put poster of Rachel Welk in barn fer to get son to do chores, up production, and teech cows humilititty.

March 12: Wife complanes of hart murmur. I told her to turn up the TV.

March 13: Went to barbers, where he told jokes made my hair stand on end. He sez it's eezier to cut that way.

March 14: Eggs down agin. Put sine in henhouse, "A aig a day keeps Kernel Sandy away."

March 15: Salivation Army come by for our cast-off clothing, but we only cast it off at nite.

March 16: Wife sez we're both gittin' Middle Ages spred. Told her it makes us even closer.

March 17: Guvmint warns us to be more gross about our national producks.

March 18: Son tells me I'm inseecure, becuz I ware both belt and suspenders.

March 19: Wife thinks she's fat, after Minister looked strait at her during a sermon on "The Flesh, that Peculyer Tempel of Plessure."

March 20: Spring tomorrow, but you kin still rite yer name in the snow.

March 21: Yer Verminal Equalnux. First sine of spring was son behind barn smokin' ceder bark.

March 22: Son gives up ceder bark. Will wate till next munth and try clover heds.

March 23: Wife helps out at Sale of Work fer the Sick and Tired of the Pressedbyteerian Church.

March 24: Wife wants to go to a Helth Farm and redooce. Wot's so unhelthy about this farm?

March 25: Rain. Wife rote pomes as it was too wet to plow.

March 26: Son got stuck in snake fence. We tried greesin his eers, got desprit, ended up cuttin' his hair.

March 27: Wife dun exorsizes before chores. Went down to cows with her face the culler of a shrimp's cock tale.

March 28: Large dog folleyed wife into phone booth in town. Neether of them cud git back out. Tuk door off.

March 29: Wife still thinks she's bulky. Told her it wernt notissable unless she's taking sumthing out of the oven.

March 30: Wife goes on diet. Nothin but black coffee and food.

March 31: Son finished his hocky seeson with 11 ghouls and I dunno how many cysts.

THOT FER THIS MUNTH

I know what I'm giving up fer Lent this year . . . all them New Year's rezzlutions I made.

SOLER ENERGY

Now that them Arbs has us over a barl, and we're gittin' short of fossilfools –purty soon even coal will be a anthrasite fer sore eyes–mebbe we shud git some substitoot fer wat's been comin out of the ground fer the last millenema or so.

Of corse, yer nukuler fizzicists told us that by this time we'd be gittin our heet from them atomical reactionaries. But peeple are startin to git leery of that way of warmin things up. Even some of the scientificks therselves are afraid one of ther piles mite go off accidental.

So mebbe it's time to go back to the center of things, and start storin up ultry-violence from its orignal sorce. Why not git off our Soler's plexus enuff energy fer to be used post-datedly insted of radio-actively?

They say we cud store up enuff in about a week-and-a-haff fer to do us the hole winter. But there's one disadvantedge to this as far as the guvmint's conserned. No refleckshun on them, but the sun comes to us direck without no middleman in between. In other words you can't put tax on yer sun like you can wen you bring up yer gas or yer oil.

I figger the only other way to keep warm is to start diggin' downward. Start bilding groundscrapers instedda sky-scrapers, and burro like a mole. Stay below, and keep in heet the way them animals do, the hole hibernation of them. It's either that, or Science Friction.

ANUTHER ANSWER TO YER ENERGY FALL-OUT

It's the horse, of corse. You mind that Sexy-rotariat, the greatest race horse since Man-a-Whore? They retired him to stud at six years old and he's still outstanding in his feeld. Thats the kind of retiremint program I always wanted. But then I found out they do his hole thing by artifishul insinuation. It seems a shame to bottle up a good draft horse.

But it jist shows you how the world is going thru the changes. If there was anything that was gradually becoming obsoleet a few yeers ago, it was yer small farmer and yer big horse. But after yer Shoddy Arabian gas attacks, and yer world food shortedge we're both back in the runnin. Speshully yer quadrupeed. If we have to git around without yer infernal combustin injin, the only thing we got to fall back on is our horse's. And I know them environmental mentalists sez that you don't intirely avoid pollyution with a horse, but at leest you can see it. And it sure comes in handy on yer peony bushes.

A Well Bred Face. *A Low Bred Face.*

MUNIPISSIPLE ELECTIONS

If you want to know what's shakin round our parts come this time of yeer it's mostly hands. The politishuns are puttin the glad finger on us as we go to the poles to exercise our french-fries.

I herd someone say that what pollyticks needs today is men of convictions, but you have to git them outa jail first. Some of them candidates boasts about startin out without a dime in ther pockets, but it don't take them too long before they discovers other peeple's pockets.

But it's the speeches gits me down. Before some of them long-winders comes to a full stop, they have put me in a comma. One speeker said after a hour and a haff that he was talkin to generations yet unborn. I figgered if he didnt git on with it they'd be here before he finished. And then everybuddy clapped him and sed it was a speech fer the ages. Sure–ages 5 to 12. Then he had the gall to ask us all to vote fer him and good govermint. He otta know we're not allowed to vote twice.

YER SPRING BROKE

This is the time of yeer the teechers lets the kids outa school fer a cuppla weeks, jist to let us know what it's like having an addled-lessent around mosta the time. Mind you, the kids don't wanta hang around. My boy Orville wants to thumb hisself all the way down to Fort Loddy-dale fer to watch all them little teeny blobbers in ther bikaneeny bathin soots (two bandaids and a plug).

I blame yer Spring Catlog fer this. Every winter wen it comes, it stirs up a lotta unrest in yer yung with them pitchers of girls in ther bald-briggand undyware. Now, in my day we used to git rid of that feelin' by goin' out and cuttin' a cord of kindlin. I'm thinkin of puttin in Orville's porritch that stuff they used to give us to make us never mind the girls in World War Eleven. But that salty-peeter takes a wile to work. I took it thirty-five yeer ago and the wife thinks the stuff is finaly startin to work.

Rite now Orville's off down the road to where they have a commune. Buncha yung hippy-optimists from the sitty tryna live off the land instedda the guvvermint. He's over there now, heevin stones fer them before they start ther harrowing days. I dunno why he can't git the rocks off at home.

YER BIRTHDAY FORTCHUNE AND GUIDE

If you were ever born
MARCH 21 up til APRIL 20
Yer astrological sine is AIRACE
Yer ruling planit is MARSE

THE YEAR AHEAD FOR ALL AIRACES: Kerb yer impatients or you will lead a dog's life. This is yer yeer to go to seed, but it may be harrowing at first. Keep wits about you, as many as possible, fer you will be in need of a laff or two. Later, yer Venis starts to rise, but as ever, duty calls. When yer Solar plexus gits restless, it will be time fer yer moon to shine. But keep still in the basement. And try to keep the law upstairs.

AIRACE brings you to yer sine of yer Ram Parts. This is one of yer Cardinals. (Nuttin' to do with ancient Grease, Rome or Saint Louis.) Do you mind the story of Jason and his Argonuts goin after yer Golden Fleas? Well sir, it was yer Ram started that old skin game, and has bin immoralized fer it ever since.

Yer Ram is a Marshal type, ruled by Marse, yer Wore God, and they butt in where they feel like. Yer Airace don't pay too much mind to his mind. After all, a Ram's best frend is his In-stink. They allus foller it, sometimes so fast they cut therselves. You can allus tell an Airace by the band-ades. If Murkry is rising in Piskey's house at yer berth, it makes yer Airace sloe-witted and fergitful. They are not too sharp, so keep them away from knives.

Some Airaces never grow up, and become seenile delinkwents. But without them we woulda never had that pineneer spirit wich makes us what we have become today.

GOOD POINTS: Fulla beans, and curridge, and sexy in a fast way.

NOTSOGOOD POINTS: Pushy, rood, selfish. They'd trample anyone fer to git to the top, and on the way sell ther grammother fer cab-fare.

PLANTERRY INFLOOENCE: On accounta yer planit Marse, yer Airace is hot and dry. Strongly affected by plants on Erth too, like thissles, ginjer, garlick, and anything with prickills.

LOOKS: Red-faced, big shoulders, black hare, liddle eyes but peercing. High foreheds and it says in a old book, "long wooly snouts," but it don't say wether yer wool is inside yer snout er out.

LOVE: One of the reesons yer Airace has a red face, is his altitude to sex. It's "wam-bam-without-even-a-thank-you-Mam". They sure don't like to hang around and chew the fat. Fer that matter they should avoid Vertgos who rubs agin Airace yer wrong way. Avoid Cansir and Crappycorn too. Commit marridge with Aquahairyass or Jiminy.

HELTH: Heddakes are freakwent doo to loss of blud. Eat lotsa termaters fer to git back yer hole ruddy complection. Also ruebarb should be took regler fer to keep the same way.

LUCKY STONE: Bloodstone. Nacherly. Also dymond (because the carrats is good fer you.)

CULLER: Red. What else? Fer day wear, why not a nicely taylered butcher's apron after you have given a hen a rinse? Also white and blue wich with red makes yer Airace pat-erotic.

FLOWRS: Bigoanya and anenemy. Mebbe butterdcups and twolips.

REEDING: Pirate storys. (a lot happens under yer skull and crotch bones.)

MUSICILL TASTE: Millinery marches.

HOBBY: Moving frum place to place . . . They rest less.

LUCKY DAY: Chewsdy. (A meat-full day.)

LUCKY NUMBER: 8. (watch it behind them balls, tho'.)

TENDENCY: Impulsivness. Also sumtimes Re-.

FAMOUS AIRACES: Yer Red Barn (him what shot down all them Slopwith Camels.) Tomas Jefferson (he wrote out the Declaration of his Dependents.) Vince Van Go (yer one Ear-ace painter.) Wermer van Brawn (the Kraut helped us git our rocks offa the moon.)

KAREERS: Any job where you git yer own way in everything. If you are not made boss first off, eggsplane you are a leeder. Be insertive, and you will carve yer way, fer Airaces is the Tarsans of yer Sodyack. They need noisy danger fer to keep them on ther mettle. A good hour of knife-sharpening before dinner will cam ther nerves. They make good foundery workers, butchers, stage mothers, quarl pickers, nite workers, and part-time lecherers.

CHARLIE'S DALY DIAREE

April 1: Yer foolsday. Tax form come, and wife still on hunger strike sept at meeltimes.

April 2: Whitewashed chicken house. Went to vet's fer dis-temperd shot.

April 3: Hurrycane wether . . . got knocked down so many times felt like the back wall of a squarsh cort.

April 4: More wind, and wet. Chased wife's new hat haff mile down the road. Turned out to be nayber's Rode Iland Red rooster. Must git glasses checked.

April 5: Son don't wanna be farmer as he has worked this place since he was born. Ast him what it was he done the first year. Told me he helped his mother with the milkin.

April 6: Water rising. Sorce of irrigation to everybuddy.

April 7: Water now rising more than yer cost of living index.

April 8: Flood. No dikes. Unexpected happens wen you leest expeck it.

April 9: Water up to the first floor winders. Wife and son in bathroom with toothbrushes waitin fer the Crest.

April 10: Son and I float out winder on dining-room table. Wife acompaninnies us on the py-anna.

April 11. Flood waters reseed quicker'n my gums. Got ague. Shakin like a cornstarch puddin.

April 12: Pigs wallering in mud. But refuse ther food. Jist bristle at it.

April 13: I refuse to nuckle to pigs, after they broke out of pen.

April 14: Spring will cum sez wife. Chin up, but watch out fer the clothesline.

April 15: Worked too hard. Dunno why I overtax myself when the guvmint does it for me.

April 16. Pigs still won't eet. Wife tired of heering me talk slop.

April 17: Wife off her feed fer a munth now. Lookin' scrawny. It used to be wen she walked, she rippled, and wen she sat down she splashed.

April 18: Daylite slavin starts soon. That meens we have our first two meels in the dark.

April 19: Wife wants to be sofisticated. Practises breethin thru her nose.

April 20: Son sez he wants to live off the land n' catch all his own food. If he'll sit still his mother will throw it at him.

April 21: Wife is happy. Found book "How to dyet wile eeting purt neer everything set in frunt of you."

April 22: Me, I eets what I like, and let the food fite it out wen it gits inside.

April 23: Son got spring feever agin. Makes him bout as useful as a crosseyed fella with a garden hose.

April 24: Gittin' spring feever myself. Feel an active old man fer my age. Wife thinks I'm a aged old man fer my act.

April 25: Back to the Land Day. Mind how you drive the spredder wen the wind changes.

April 26: Guvmint comes back from Eester reecess, reddy to lay more aigs.

April 27: Had a fair spell. Felt dizzy during it.

April 28: Everybuddy round here pritty well into ther Stanley Cups.

April 29: Church supper. Wife sez I disgraced myself by eeting sellery. Sounded if I was steppin' on a six-quart basket.

April 30: Saw my first robbin of the yeer. Two fellas held up a gas station.

THOT FER THIS MUNTH

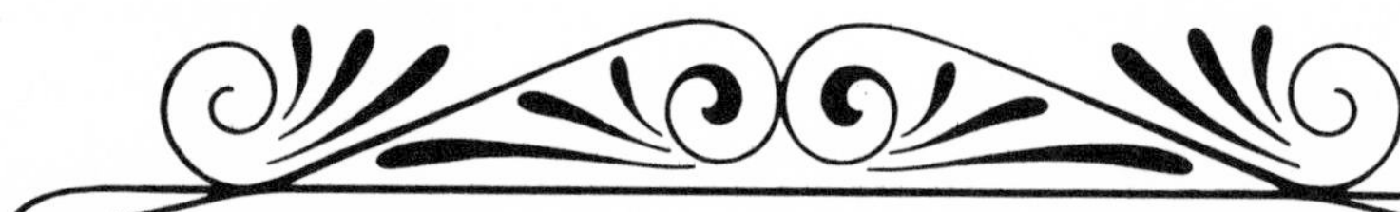

Cost of keepin' up living is still increasing. Don't take any wooden dimes!

All you do is Sit and Sprinkle.

EASTER

Are you one of them twice-a-yeer church goers? Was the last time you bowed yer hed at the Candle lit-up service at Chrissmus? All Easter meens to a lotta peeple is bunnies and chicks. Lookin in the stores you'd think Hugh Heffer was in charge of it. We never had choclit-dipped rabbits wen I was a tad. Oh, we tried it once, but them rabbits kep squirmin too much wen we dipped them in the hot choclit.

But Easter gits a lotta peeple to church, sittin ther in ther new Easter ensembles. (That's French fer havin all yer close on.) I don't think it matters much wat gits you to church, jist sittin' there with yer head bowed is gonna do good, even if it jist meens lettin' the blood rush back to yer frontle low-bottomies.

Farmers stick closer to the church than most, I spose. If you got seed in the ground, you know there's nothin much you kin do about it before hoein, except hemmin and hawin. So you mite as well git down on yer knees and ask fer a little help. But remember to give thanks fer last yeer's harvest too. Most peeple only git on ther knees nowadays to change the Chanel on the TV. I go every week becuz the wife is second mezzanine in the choir soprannas. I love to heer her sing "Leed Kinda Lightly" and "Oblige With Me." It's harder to drag our boy out. He stays out Sardy nites dancin. He'd rather rock fer ages than come to church and sing about it. Seems to me yung peeple today are more intrusted in the fella with the horns. Everybuddy went to that movie the "Ex-orsesassasist" where the devil got busted fer possessyun. But my boy he don't bleeve in the devil neether. He says it's jist like Sandy Claws, it always turns out to be yer own father.

Th'other day he said to me: "Dad, you tole me our church has bin here fer purt neer two thousand yeer, and jist lookit the state of the wirld today!"

I told him. I said: "Orville-water has bin around fer more'n two billion year–and jist lookit the state of yore neck!"

CAPITALIST'S PUNISHMENT

Yas, it's incum tax time agin, wher they have to burn us fiscally fer to make ther ends meet. I thot it was bad enuff what they charge me last yeer, but there's bin an offal lotta water over the mill-rate since. Never mind figgerin out how much profet you made last year. Yer jist holdin it fer the guvmint between colleckshuns.

You jist can't win. If you do wrong, they fine you. If you do right, you pay that much more in taxes anyway. I dunno why a slite tax increese comes to a cuppla hundred dollers per anum, wile a substanchle tax cut is mebbe 2 or 3 cents.

It's pritty sneeky the way they git you to hand in yer tax money before they brings out the budget and tells you how they're gonna spend it. I think it takes more time tryna figger out what you owe the Infernal Revenooers than it takes to go out and ern it. Last yeer wen I was makin out the Declaration of my Dependents, the wife remind me about that rash of hives we had at strawbury time last yeer. The hole famly cum down with a regler epidermis, cost me 75 dollers. So I put down fer expenses "Hives $75." Well, I must a put it in the wrong place cuz six months later I got a letter sayin: "Re: Hives $75. Kindly send detales on revenue from bee-keeping." I think I'll take up bee-keeping now. I bin stung every other way there is.

Sumtimes you kin git a reprobate on yer tax, if you have an accountant who knows how to make a tax shelter fer yer reclining yeers, and is something of a Master Rebator. But then yeers later they can git back at you with RollOver. That's a Re-asses-essment of yer back taxes. It sounds like something that happens to a dog, but it shoodn't. Jist wen you think yer in clover, they take you out, lay you down, and do it agin.

Sometimes I think it'd be better if I jist sent them my incum and kept the tax. This yeer they told me I cud pay by the quarter, so I sent them off the 25 cents and I hope it holds them fer a wile.

DAYLITE SLAVIN'

Wen I was a boy, we didn't have to set out fer scool durin yer Dark Ages. But nowadays, wen even Time has gone off the Standerd, it seems we're workin the gravy-yard shift at both ends. It don't make no never mind to me . . . I git up in the dark anyways all yeer round. A lotta peeple ask me if I ever wake up Grouchy at that time. I tell them, no, I always let her sleep another fifteen minits.

ADVERTISEMENT

RENDER CONSTIPATION TERMINAL
FIG YOURSELF TO FREEDOM.

Don't go off half-caulked but
Make your morning toilet

A HAPPY OCCASION

YER BIRTHDAY FORTCHUNE AND GUIDE

If you were ever born
APRIL 21 up til MAY 21
Yer astrological sine is TOARASS
Yer ruling planit is VEENIS

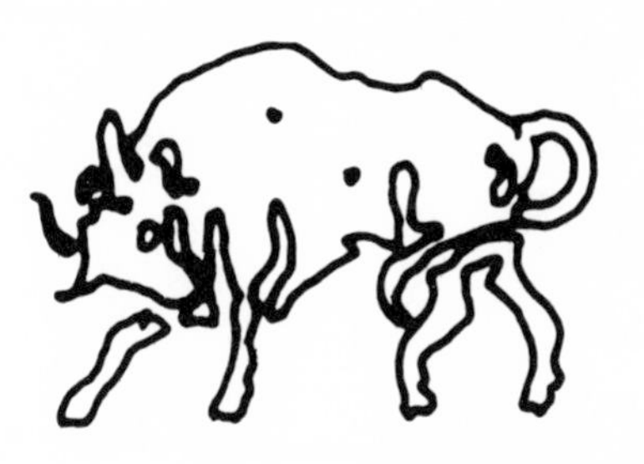

THE YEAR AHEAD FOR ALL TOARASSES: At the first of this yeer, yer still in the doll-drums of the nite-house of Venis. This meens yer not up to much till them little croakus starts to git pushy. By this time you'll be snortin' fer action, but hold yerself till the grass is dry. May to September is yer time to snort n' bellow. After that, pull in yer horns agin, and try to unravel with travel.

TOARASS is yer sine of yer Bull, stable and fixed. But my gol, what good in the stable is a fixed Bull? And don't talk to me about artyfishul incrimination. No cow is gonna settle fer that bottled stuff so long as she kin still git draft.

Toarass is one of yer most Erthy sines, as anybody knows who has had to spread it around.

Yer Toarasses sure like ther roots. They is pritty much sticky-at-homes, like to rap therselves in ther secure-titty blanket. If you git invited to a Toarass dinner, R.S. yer V.P. D.Q. because they sure groan a good board. They likes to live good, have nice things around them (like fresh straw in ther stalls).

They is slow to git mad, but look out if they see red. They starts to snort thru ther nose and paw the turf. A Toarass on his ram-page is hell on weels. Any bull-fitter (what they call down to Mexico yer Matted-Door) can tell you not to rush yer Toarass neether.

PLANITERRY INFLUENTS: If you got Murkry in yer Toarass, ain't nuthin' gonna move you. Them borned closer to Jiminy is looser and more flecksibble. Veenis gives Toarass its infenctionate looks. They sure know how to love. But after, they like to put the loved one in a glass case, like yer objay darts (that's French fer things you keep locked up).

GOOD POINTS: Steddy, truss-worthy, infectionit, relye-a-bull.

BAD POINTS: Jellus, hates to be counter-dicted, stubbern, boring, and pissessiv.

LOVELIFE: Yer Toarass is erly develpers and on first dates tends tord ravishes. But they is loil, prooves to be steddy rapers, and after rooteen, becums more coshus. They also have good rithm, wich helps if you are Cathlick.

FAMLY: Wen it comes to kids, Toarasses is old-fashioned pairints, and lays on hevvy with the dissaplin. Toarasses has good voice boxes and kin shout loudern anyone else. This helps raisin' kids, but puts a strain on yer generation's gap.

LOOKS: Toarasses is sposed to be the best lookin', as long as you don't mind the tipe that walks slow, looks down at yer erth, and chews ther cud a lot. They are good heds genrully, with strong necks and jaws, ferm mouth, bulbus eyes, the odd tuft of hair on ther foreheads, and wide nostrils, so's the person that gives them a ring kin lead them by the nose.

HELTH: Hevvy in yer throat, kidnees and lumber reegions. They kin avoid hoofin'mouth by keeping ther traps shut. Toarasses make good wate-lifters, wich is jist as well since they love good food and have to work it off somehow. They shud eat beans fer ther complection, and sellery fer to clear out their systern. (Ya'd think the beans would do that.) By the bye, some Toarasses is perferts, and even impa-tint. (This is a gud combination. Keeps them outa trouble.)

MARRIDGE AND DEEVORCE: Hook up with Vertgo, Crappycorn or Piskeys, but stay away frum yer Leeos and yer Aquahairyass. Toarasses tend to be pissessiv after deevorce, and may demand custidy of ex-husband.

LUCKY JOOL: Emmrild. (Lucky fer yer Toarass. Not so lucky fer them as has to give it to them.)

CULLERS: Yer pink and yer pastells. (Fer a bull? Told ya it was fixed.)

FLOWRS: Vilet, dazey, junk-will and yer tailing arbrutus.

REEDING: Sumthing roemantick with a hint of rape.

MUSICK: Classyfied consert played by sympathy orkester. (Like yer Bluebeerd of Happyness.)

HOBBY: Handy Kraft. (How to make it manyally with cheese.)

LUCKY DAY: Frieday.

LUCKY NUMBER: Sex.

BEST PLACES: Feelds. Altho Toarasses think more of ther future, it's hard to put them out to pasture.

BIGNAME TOARASSES: Karl Marx (he saw Red). Sweet Willyum Shakespeer (Avon calling). Sigma Freud (invented the number sex). Irvin Berlin (wrote both words and lyrics All Ways).

KAREER: Toarasses handle money well, but who kin make a living fondling the stuff? They make good archy-tecks (strong out-bildins) rich farmers, (most aggerculture is based on Bull) and most of all, singers with deep throtes.

DOWN WITH BLOOD!

Beware that Headlong Rush!!

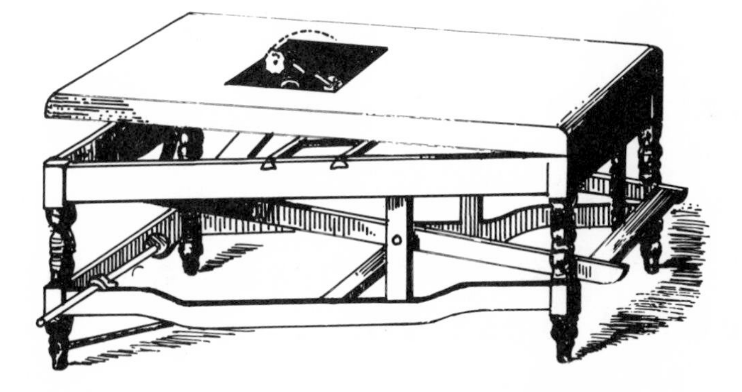

Lying with the head lower than the feet causes giddiness, sometimes even hysteria. This can happen during sleep and give rise to wanton dreams. Put the blocks to the upper portion of your body with Marter's Cork Triangular Bed Wedge. Guarantees a flow of blood to your feet at all times. A missionary writes: Marter's block is the best thing for a man in my position.

MAKE YOUR OWN GAS

at a cost of a few cents a week.

NO WICKS • NO ODOR • NOTHING SACRED OR PROPANE

Will send you a small model [five-foot-three] to enable you to start at full pressure.

Nothing to get out of order.

Send us the money and you will get the shaft.

MARSHALL GAS CO. **Okefenokee Swamp, Flas.**

CHARLIE'S DALY DIAREE

May 1: Mayday, mayday. Holyday in Moscow. Harrowing day here. Heeving my stones as I go.

May 2: Gittin more rocks off. As out of wind as a bowlegged tuber player in a marchin' band.

May 3: Wife sees my breth comin in short pants. Feels I have let myself go. (And enjoyed it both times.)

May 4: Found out wife has kept all her aig money in her mattress so she'll have sumthin to fall back on.

May 5: Got took by wife to lecher on culcher. Not agri or horta, jist plain. Had about as much fun as a vegy-taryan vampire.

May 6: Wife's berthday. She's in her late erly forties.

May 7: Mother's Day. Combine gifts by givin her a little oven erly in the morning.

May 8: Wife wants new dish-washer. I ast her what I was doin' wrong.

May 9: Girl on next farm gits engaged. Famillyarity breeds consent.

May 10: Son sings in barn to kill time. He has a devastaitin weppon.

May 11: Our cow give berth to quadruppeds. Must phone Bull of the Munth club.

May 12: Hospiddle wants test for suger. Staid up all nite studying for it.

May 13: Hospiddle sez magnificent spessimen. Passed test with flying cullers.

May 14: Cot a draft from them backward minny-skirt gowns.

May 15: Staid in town fer a bit, watching yung girls go past. Paid no mind to old wives' tails.

May 16: Son late fer dinner agin. Wife says he has a body that wanders without his mind.

May 17: Wife gits a touch of ruematiz from damp blowse, crying on phone over other peeple's trubbles.

May 18: Saw an Alfalfa Romeeo go by–furrin sports car forty foot long, mebbe nine inches high.

May 19: Son wants to go to town, see moovy "Deep Throat." Sez it's a Walt Dizzly moovy about sick giraffs.

May 20: Wife found out that moovy is about oral sex. What good is talkin about it the day after?

May 21: Wife back to her exorsizes. Standing snatch. That's touching yer nees without bendin the floor.

May 22: Wife pulled at her feet fifteen minits every hour. In a munth her shoe size will go from six to eight.

May 23: I sneezed after eetin a mouth fulla sponge cake. Wife hadda cleen the hole house.

May 24: Wife buys plastick cover to keep over me wen I 'm not in use.

May 25: Wife making costooms fer Strawbury Festivall. Give her the tulle and she'll finish the job.

May 26: Our son restless. Sumtimes goes without sleep all day.

May 27: Travellin' sailsmen drop in. Them fellers cud sell bagels in Shoddy Arabia.

May 28: Got cot in rushour in town. Well, I s'pose it's faster than crawlin' home on hands and nees.

May 29: Somebuddy has bot the tellyfone booth on Main Street and is openin it as a earing boo-teek.

May 30: Mimmorial Day. Tried on my old War II unyform. Only part still fit was the tie.

May 31: Nayber's girl give shower. Groom-to-be says feeling is nupptual. He first made her acquaintints wen his contack lens fell in her cleevedge.

THOT FER THIS MUNTH

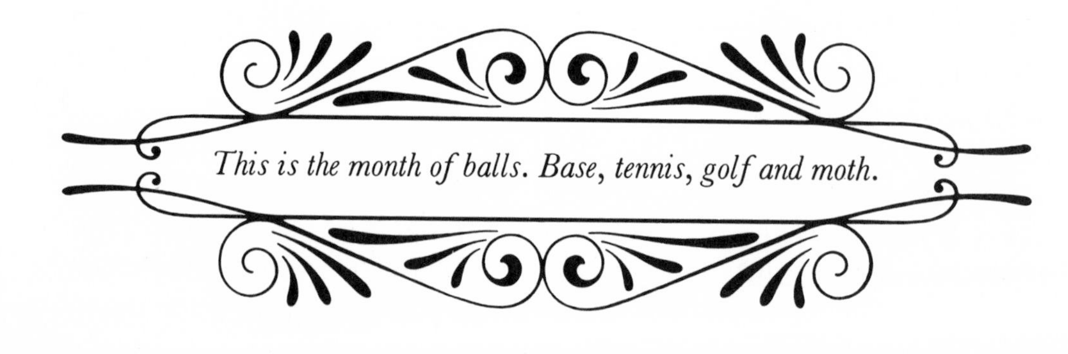

This is the month of balls. Base, tennis, golf and moth.

STARTING RITE WITH SHEEP

And Working yer Way up Two Candles

Dipping yer wick is not that differnt from doin it to a sheep or a candle, except that the latter can be dun in the privacy of yer own home.

There is jist no tellin wat can be done with yer sirplus animal fat. And not jist animal. We all have a little waist fat around ourselfs. But it comes eezier offa yer heffer or ewe. All you need is a fifty-gallin tub or barl, a paira rubber boots and a sheep, with a faucet neer the bottom (of yer barl er tub).

Sheep care takes mebbe ten minits a day. They don't fite back. Sheep are basickly chicken, wich is why they are called sheep. But they take care of you, too. They are nature's trimmers, freeks fer grass. There is nothing a sheep likes more than to have a good crop on yer lawn. And fer dessert they likes poison ivy. What more cud you ask?

A sheep's only perteckshun is its fleas. There is sheer joy in fleesing a sheep, and after yer fleesircus must come the dip, fer to git rid of them interminable paris-ites. Ther tail shud be cut off erlier (See Docking Proceedures). Otherwise a sheep kin foul itself, wich is a pen-yard penalty. Sheeps without tails are called wethers, on accounta they are not too sure of therselves after that.

Try a sheep dip at yer next party. But it can't hold a candle to doing it yerself. You don't need a sheep, jist make use of them fat scraps you have at home with the wife.

All you need fer wick-dipping is a big pot, a cheesy cloth so you'll strain yerself, and a long-handled spoon fer gettin' down to it. And tallow–tallow is jist fat wich has bin Rendered under Seizure, as the Good Book says. You kin even git it from bull's rushes if you soak the pith out of them. (Creckshun: thoak the pith out of them.)

Moulds fer candles kin cum from anywheres. Used toilet rolls is good but spray them first with sillycones so's they won't stick to yer wick. Before dippin yer wick in the melted tallow, boil the hole of it in alum first fer to tighten her up, then soak in salty-peeter fer to make it slack agin. Then chill the hole bizness overnite and in the morning lift off the hardened fat. This applys to both candles and sheep. They both works good in a energy crisis, becuz neether has to be plugged into the wall, or fit with a shade. Candles is no trubble but sheep is more fun.

But first get to know yer sheep. Git wise to them in ther ways. Remember it's up to you to make the first move. Without touching on the fundymentals, it takes a trained hand to feel them out. Better still–keep two sheep fer they love to flock and soon becum pen pals.

HAS CLUMBUS HAD HIS DAY?

Histerians is now finding out that Norse Amerka wasn't uncovert by Columbus at all. Turns out our continence got foundered even before 1942 by some Porchgeese fishymen who kept rowin further'n further away from ther home town of Porchgull to drop ther hooks. First they hit them islands jist a ways out in yer Altantis–yer Canarys, and yer A-Sores. By n' by they wound up over our way. By the time Clumbus was settin' out on his Carrybean crooze with his four maiden voyeurs, Nina, Pinto, Sandy and Maria, these Porchgeese hookers had bin hanging around the Grand Banks of Newfyland fer a cod's age.

So why didn't we heer about it before? Well, that's yer avridge fishyman. He don't mind boastin' bout the ones got away, but as soon as they starts to bite he'll clam up like a erster. A cupple of them Porchgeese, Fiasco the Gambla and Madge Ellen circumsized the hole erth without tellin nobody.

But back even before yer Porchgeese was yer Vikings, big blond sailers from the Scandalnavya, with horny hats. They used to sneek over to Iceland week-ends fer to git some, and lay waist. Now this'd be about 1000 B.B.C. (Back Before Clumbus).

One of them, Eric yer Red, got as fur as Massachewsits. Nobuddy knows how long he staid, but he still has famly livin' hard by today. You probly herd of yer Road Iland Reds.

DID YER MOTHER CUM FROM ICELAND WITH A LITTLE BIT OF HERRING?

Nowadays, we're finding out that somebuddy beet yer Viking to the punch. And if it's anybody that's first to yer punch at a party it's yer Irishman. I know, because my incesters is all Ulcermen from Bellyfast.

Happened about yer Anal Domino 545, not too long after yer Deecline and Fall-out from yer Roamin Umpire. A sainted preest name of Brendan went out in his little round bottom bote, and went island hoppin' without missin a one–Yer Orknees–yer Fairyos–yer Shatlands–on to yer Ice and Green Lands, yer Newfy, Yer Road, even yer Stattin too. Then a shortspin over to Bermooda, and ended up on yer Grand Banana hard by Nasser.

And you have to bleeve him, becuz saints don't tell no fibs or they don't git cannonaded. Now there's no writ proof of this, becuz us Irish is vurry oral about our histry, and can't be botherd puttin' it down anually. But there is took-down prufe that us Irish got to where Clumbus was aimin' at–yer Fur Eest–long before any other Yerpeen.

One of our fellers in his Middle Ages, went past the canals of Venis, past yer Asian Miners, over yer Go-bye Desert til he ended up in Far Camay, at the plessure dome of yer Grate Can, the hed Pekinese. He brot back some spicy storys you kin still reed today.

And what was this broth of a boy's name? None of yer furrin monickers like Clumbus. He was one of our own Irish lads, Mark O'Poly-o.

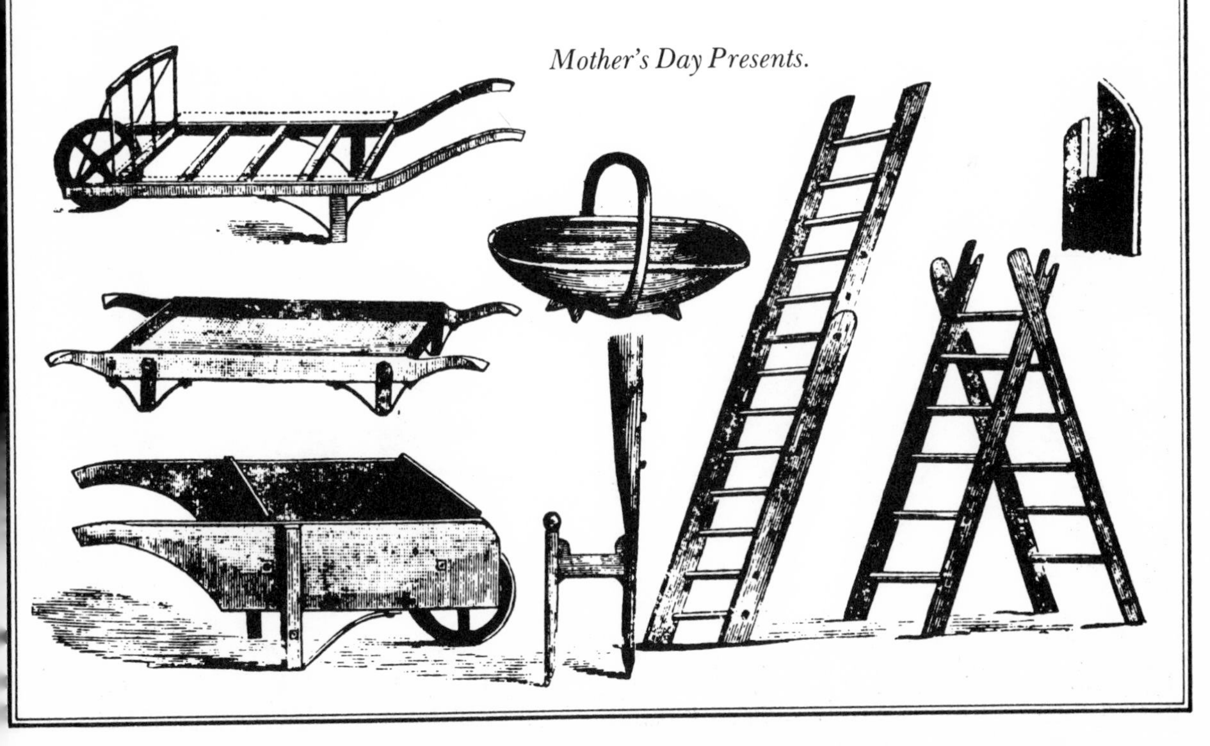

Mother's Day Presents.

YER BIRTHDAY FORTCHUNE AND GUIDE

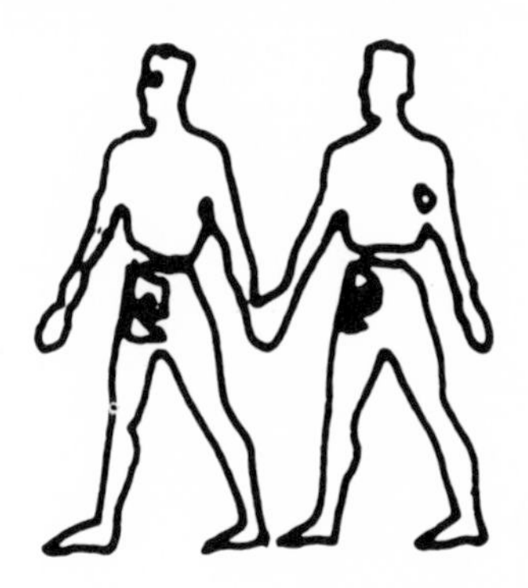

If you were ever born
MAY 22 up til JUNE 21
Yer astrological sine is JIMINY
Yer ruling planit is MURKRY

THE YEAR AHEAD FOR ALL JIMINIES: Now listen, both of you . . . git yer heads outa the sand and use that good old-fashind grit. You've had yer whoopee fer a wile. It's time to close the door on adverse developmints. Expeck to rate later in the year. Help from unexpected sorcers in September. By October you may git a windfall. (Don't eat. Sell!)

JIMINY is dubble or nuthin' . . . playin' both sides of the street at the same time . . . this two-headed munster is seen up in the sky every nite as Casterer and Pole-axe, a pair of kids (the kind from which you git yer gote) that make up two of yer britest stars in the hevvily constipations.

That's Jiminy all right, a mixed-up pare of kids can't make up ther minds wich one is the leeder, yer nanny or yer horny. That's because Jiminy is what they call yer Mute-able sine, always goin' thru the changes, fulla speed and livin' on ther nerves (and on other peeples too).

Yer Jiminy knows how to play both its sides agin its middle, argew black is white, and then quick as Billy-o change sides without missin' a stroke. The quick parts comes from Murkry, yer god of flowrs delivered by male, who is also yer patronizing saint of motor scooters and bisecksuals. Some of yer Jiminies is switch hitters both on and offa yer mound (from Veenis). And who'll look sweet, upon the seat, of a bi-secksual bilt fer two?

Jiminies also got this intelleckyule bent. They is awful good at crotchword puzzles, forn langridges, and sarcasticks. Better at wordplay than sordplay, they kin still run a few peeple thru the vowels.

GOOD ASSPECKS: Widdy, yuthfull, fulla beens, and grate at partys. (But count yer silverware after. They'll eat yer cake and have yer plate too.) But they give other peeple more of a lift than they do fer therselfs. Jiminy is a fun bunch, all two of them.

BAD ASSPECKS: Restless, jumpy, gossipy, hippycrits, and genially untrussworthy.

PLANITAIRY INFLOONCE: If yer Murkry is up in yer Jiminy's berth, look out. Everything gits frenantic and Jiminy ends up beside hisself. But if Murkry is in yer Toreass insted, Jiminy cams down and ends up stabled.

LOVE: Jiminy is yer cool cat... flirty but not dirty. And sot after on accounta ther verse-agility. (Two can think up more shinny-annigans than one.) Jiminy is attrackted to both Leeo and Airace, and will probly end up with one of eech (yer Infernal Try-angle).

FAMILY: Jiminies make grate pairints fer kids because they is both modren and tallerant. One thing frusterates Jiminies' kids, ther pairints never git offa the tellyphone. Jiminy likes a happy home on yer one hand, but gits threttend after a wile by all that stabilititty. Mebbe Jiminy should marry anuther Jiminy and the four of them cud contrack to play bridge.

HELTH: Jiminies tend to be maniac-depressivs, wich means uppers and downers at the same time. A lot of them is Vegetary Aryans, so to make up fer not gittin' much in yer red meat departmint, Jiminy shud eat lotsa carots fer to permote fertilititty. Also makes them gud at nite baseball, and other lite sports. Jiminies are best at two-part sports like yer ping and yer pong. Who's better than Jiminy wen it comes to playing with yerself?

LOOKS: Lean, long, low like a dear or a whip-it. Yer duel nature keeps you under-weight, you kin eat fer two and have a figger fer one.

LUCKY JOOLS: Ag-its. (Jiminies never lose ther marbles.)

FLOWR: Lilly-of-yer-Valley, and fer the boys, Jack-up-yer-Pullpits.

READING: Advencher storys. (somebody eltses, nacherly.)

DAY: Wen's Day.

CULLERS: Loud checks.

LUCKY NUMBERS: Five. (Jiminies shud take five wenever they can.)

TENDENCYS: Splits pursnality. Jiminies tend to fork off in all drections.

BEST LOCATIONS: High places. (bars, cock tailoungers.)

KAREER: Bein' dubble-barld, yer Jiminy kin probly hold two jobs at the same time. Since they are experts at cunning and frod, they make good travling salesmen and noosepaper jurnlists.

BIG JIMINIES: Don Wan (yer grate luvver tired hisself out, went all to Hell). Danty (anuther Eyetalian went to hell in his own way and rote yer In-furniss).
Wagner (not Robert, but Richerd, rote all that Godammerung musick like yer Dristan and I-Solder).
John Wayne (has to be a Jiminy. He's big enuff fer two).

THIS WILL
INTEREST MANY

Especially those afflicted with pain leading to social embarrassment. Send your address to me at my Box (1501 Boston Mass.) and I will direct you to someone who will let you off this burden. I have nothing to sell or give, just tell you how I was cured. Complete confidence. I have always been known as a Confidence man. Think of me as someone who wishes to share his troubles with you.

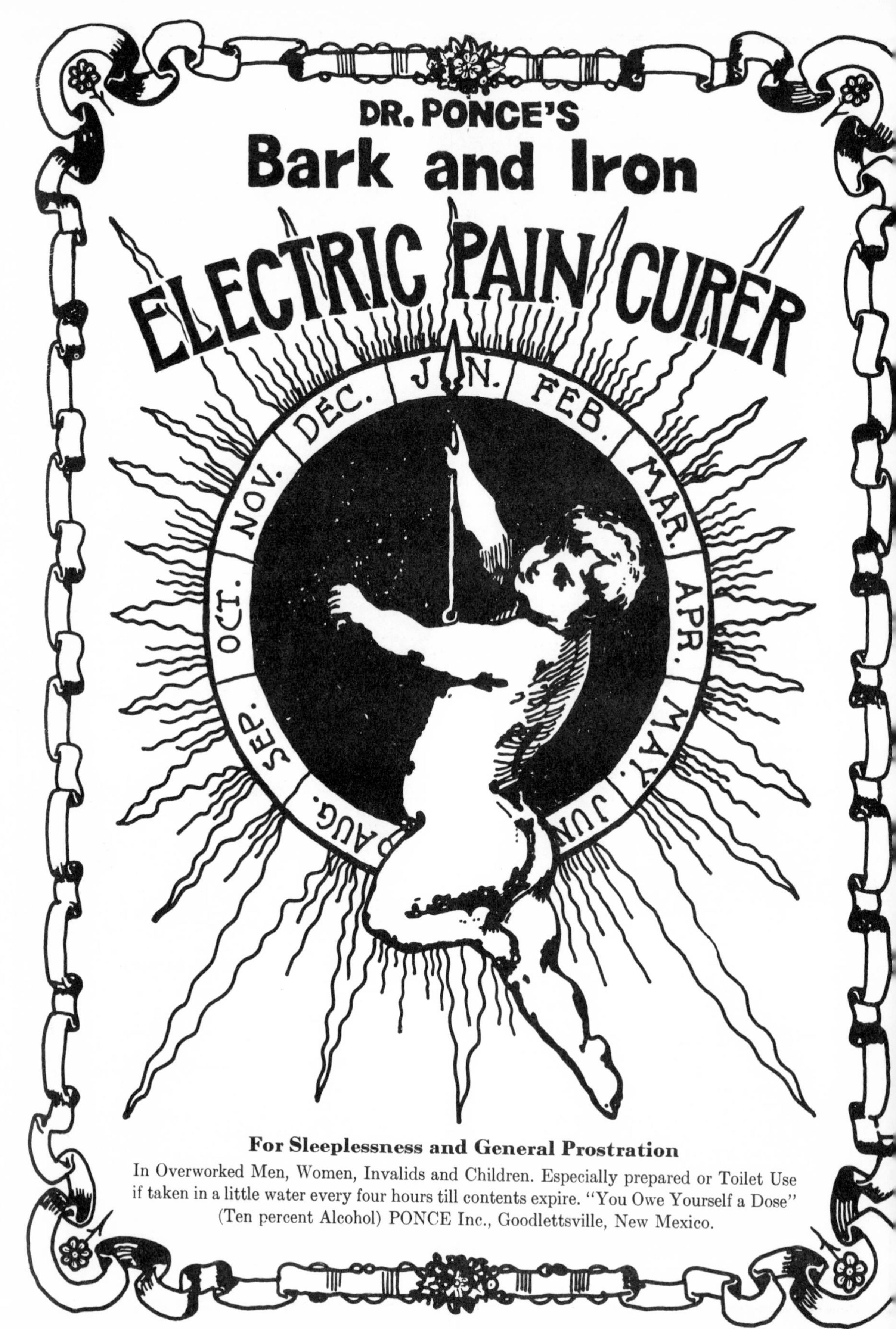
DR. PONCE'S
Bark and Iron
ELECTRIC PAIN CURER
JAN. FEB. MAR. APR. MAY. JUN. AUG. SEP. OCT. NOV. DEC.
For Sleeplessness and General Prostration
In Overworked Men, Women, Invalids and Children. Especially prepared or Toilet Use if taken in a little water every four hours till contents expire. "You Owe Yourself a Dose"
(Ten percent Alcohol) PONCE Inc., Goodlettsville, New Mexico.

JUNE

CHARLIE'S DALY DIAREE

June 1: Wife sez we've lost most of our cherries. Starlings.

June 2: Went to Strawberry Festerall. Watched the hives.

June 3: Wife wants a screen test. It's fly time.

June 4: Son doin better at scool. Up to 30 words a minit now. Not tiping, reeding.

June 5: Father's Day. Blest be yer ties that blind.

June 6: Inter-mitten showers. I still prefurs a bath.

June 7: Wife's brother's golden anniversery. Fifty yeers happily unmarried.

June 8: Saw a city girl hitching in her overalls. I think the end justifys the jeens.

June 9: House call fer docter. Son got his tung stuck in a coke bottle watching French moovy on TV.

June 10: Gittin' warmer. Girls walkin round stark naked frum the nees down and the shoulder blades up.

June 11: Our weddin anniversery. Fergit wich one, but brung the wife a box of palomino cherries and a heating pad.

June 12: Overwate naber of ours fell offa her henhouse roof, no one around, and she rocked herself to sleep trying to get back on her feet agin.

June 13: Son went to a party Sardy nite to preserve wild life.

June 14: Wife still on diet. Told her that if she gits an ullser, she's so skinny she'll have to hold it in her hand.

June 15: Saw a girl with a shimmy to her like a 7-foot saw with a 5-inch play, cause a 6 cart pile-up in a Soupymarket.

June 16: Nayber's girl's weddin. Didnt reelize she was such a jellus tipe. All the bridesmades was males.

June 17: Wife loves weddin deceptions. She sez marridge is a mute-chill partnership. I must be the mute.

June 18. Had my pitcher took with one of them Poler-hemmeroid cameras. Enjoyed the hot flash.

June 19: Bride will be carried over her thresh-hole by groom. After that, she'll put her foot down.

June 20. Son's report card. Teecher sez if our boy ever sed what he's thinkin', he'd be downrite speechless.

June 21: First day of summer. Last day fer our rooster. Passed over by a sports car.

June 22. Can't git sub-rooster fer six weeks. No danger of ovary-production.

June 23: Sicked dog on hens jist to take them outa therselves.

June 24: Went to see teecher about son. She says he's probly very brite but jist don't have it up here.

June 25: Like the way the wimmen dress in summer. Footloose and fanny free.

June 26: Bridled cupple home from honeymoon. Her fat mother wore a white dress and after supper they showed home moovys on her.

June 27: Groom sed bride was sick on her hunnymoon. Wat a rotten waste of a dubble room!

June 28: Preecher give sermon to us that most divorces is caused by drunkeness . . . (So is most marridges.)

June 29: Put up sine to slow down highway traffick fer our cows. "GO SLOW. NOODIST CAMP."

June 30: Playd baseball in fallow pasture. Game called when I slud into wat I thot was third base.

THOT FER THIS MUNTH

This here's the month fer graduations, weddings and babies, sometimes all happening at the same time with the same girl.

LOVIN' MARRIDGE

Ther's no doubt, June is the munth fer broads. Marridge is still the best basis fer gettin acquainted on long terms, and besides, as Emly's Post sez, it makes fer good breeding.

The thing that holds most marridges together is poverty, becuz it costs money to deevorce and even more to seprate. Sumtimes it mite be better if all the wimmen was married and all the men was single. Fer about the time wimmen start goin thru the changes, men is enterin ther second childhood. That's when a man of forty starts thinkin about changing his wife fer two twenties.

The wife and I got engaged in June, thus ending a frendship wich had begun in kindygarden. In some peeple's minds, engaged is as good as bein married. In my mind, it's better. Nowadays you hear about a yung cupple tying the knot and you figger they've probly had a vasextummy.

We went to the Harness-Kruse weddin last June. The cupple had bin engaged fer sixteen yeers, altho neether had never bin married before, at least not persnally. Gay's a town girl and one of the Main Street Kruses and her and Eldon had bin goin' together longer than the gates at the jail farm. Eldon sez he finely got married when she run out of conversation. Eldon, he likes a quiet life.

The one sad note at the weddin, was her parents, who are no longer in harness, having legally shipped out from each other. We always thot they were the perfect couple, on accounta he snores and she's deff as a post. But turns out there was a drinkin problem. She never liked him wen he got drunk, and he coodn't stand the site of her sober.

It's too bad. I think marridge is the only way to live; fer whatever happens to you in life, it's nice to have someone by yer side that you kin blame it all on.

TOORISTS

June to us is garbidge-by-the-wayside munth. That's wen city picknickers has a dump of bottles, cans and tishy paper all over our rode-sides and even our fallow feelds.

We thot of takin' down ther plate number, checkin with yer Veehicular Motors Branch, and finding out the address of them Barbercue-aryans. Then we'd pack up all ther trash and dump it back on ther lawn in the city.

But they out-number us. And now we hear that mayers of cities are trying to hire trucks fer to ship all ther crapping corruption out to where we live in the country.

If you can't beat the smotherers, join 'em. This summer we're goin' into the toorist bizness. I'm gonna have a little rode-side stand where I sell orgasmic vegibles. That's sposed to be the kind growed with natcheral fertlizer, but that's jist a lotta bull.

The wife she's gonna sell her meat pies over to the restrunt at the gas station. Then when yer toorist pulls up to the pumps to fill his tank and drane his famly, he'll smell them pies, becuz the wife throws one of the best spreads on the road. Then them toorists kin eat and get gas at the same time.

GOOD FOR WEAK LUNGS

The Mettle Tester Par Excellence!

SCREECH

The National Drink of Newfoundland

Enjoy Primal Therapy and Treat Yourself to a SCREECH

NEWFY FIRST AID CO. Dildo, Nfld.

★ (WARNING: Can take the paint off cars) ★

GOLF

My farm is next door to a golf corse. And this is the time of yeer all them strangers come up from the city, and starts hoppin over my snake fence lookin fer ther balls. Now I don't know too much about yer golf, and woodn't even know wich end of the caddy you grab aholt of. But it sure makes me laff to see them big bizness tyfoons down on ther hands and knees in my hardwood bush lookin fer a white dot in a cowflap.

Now, of corse, it's not nice to laff at the idiotsinkerseas of other peeple. I spose the wife and I look jist as foolish during the curling, with her heavin her stones down the ice and me runnin in front of them braking wind with my broom. But I don't see yer men and wimmen playin together with ther tee-caddies and club-bags. The wife and I are broom-mates and curl up and sweep together all winter. But wen warm wether comes we're too busy thrashin about in the feelds to go chasin a little ball into a hole.

And I still think it's an awful waste of a good pasture to take ten acres of timothy and punch eighteen holes in it, jist so some tired bizness man kin have a few strokes. Well, it's a nice soft green place fer to drop.

But I cud harrow that hole place with the John Dear in haff a day. Them fellers takes all summer and part of yer fall, fer to plow that up with ther tools. And they have between five and six irons, altho' they only yell "four" all the time. But golfers is congeenial lyers, everyone knows that.

Even our minister plays golf. I gess he must be gittin most of his yeer's salary in money to afford that. And he does pritty good too fer a fella that has the handycap of workin on Sundys. Prayr is the seecret he sez. The hole secret before every stroke is keeping yer hed down.

Me, I'll never be a golfer. I think the only two good balls I ever hit was the day I stepped on the garden rake by mistake.

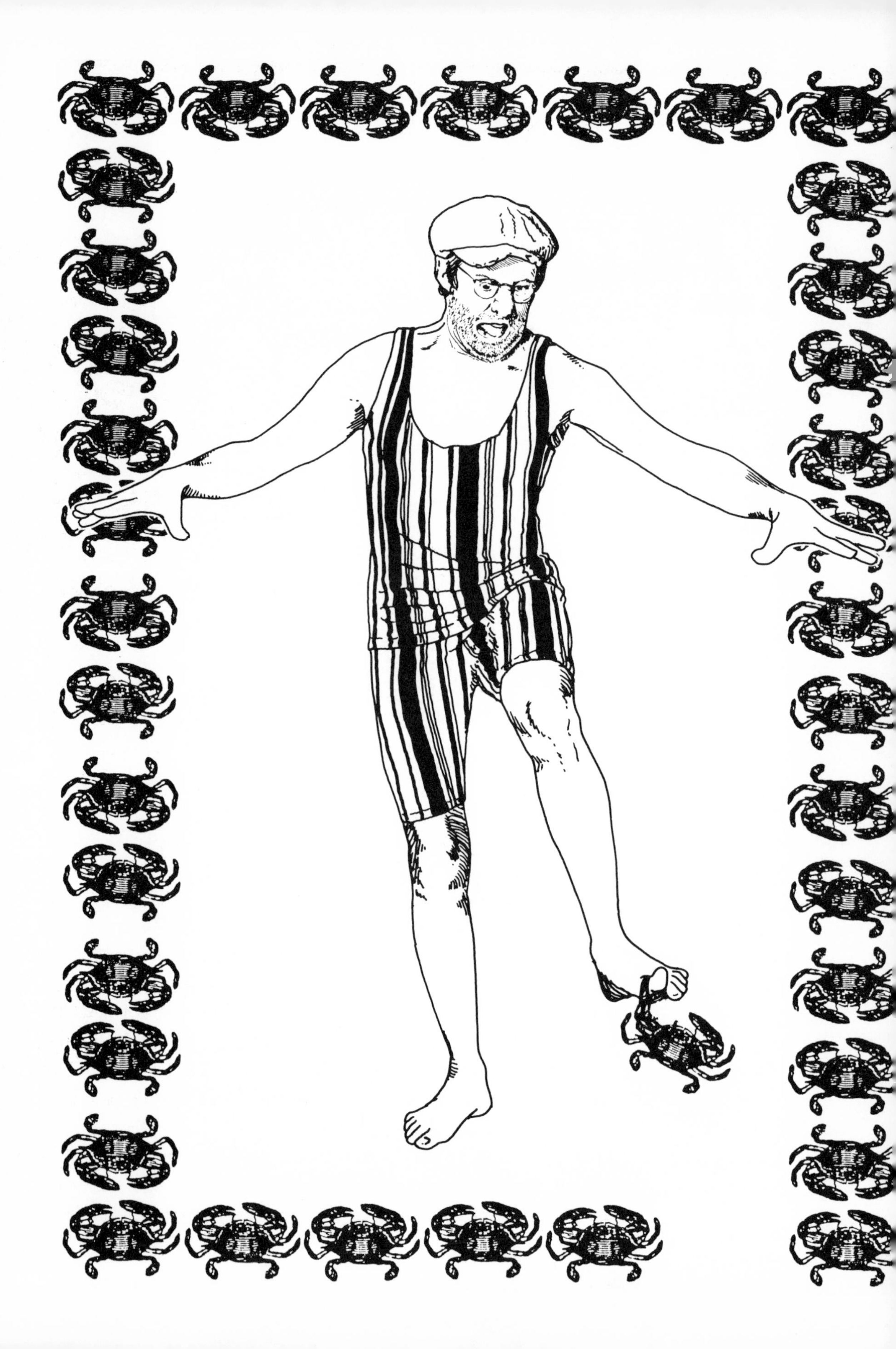

YER BIRTHDAY FORTCHUNE AND GUIDE

If you were ever born
JUNE 22 up til JULY 23
Yer astrological sine is CANSIR
Yer ruling planit is THE MOON

THE YEAR AHEAD FOR ALL CANSIRS: Yer crabby seeson starts with ruffing it, but ends in domestic bliss. Well, haff bliss, anyways. A square from Saturn bisexes the angle of yer Ruler, the Moon, and things start to perk down a bit. Second haff of the yeer, keep a tight rein in yer spending. No sweat. Sell yer home.

CANSIR is one of yer more watery sines, and states the case fer yer Crabs. That don't meen Cansirs is all that crabby . . . jist with-drawers into ther shells . . . and beneeth that shell is offen a sensativ sole and sumtimes a weak karacter. But not weak in ther morls, jist sorta soft in the hed.

Cansir is yer Mother-tipe grabber, holds on fer dear life. Reel worry worts, they make frownin' into a worka fart. A lotta Cansir men is mummy boys, and never git to come out of ther shells and snap ther claws, even tho this is the time of year, yer Summer Stallstiss, wich is big on fertililitty and contraception.

POSTIVS: Simpthetic, pertectiv, and deevoted to yer home and harth. The hole thing must sound like a mother's day card, and that's what Cansirs mostly is. (Reel mothers, not cards.)

NEGTIVS: Moony and Moody. They sit on ther grudge and hold it frever. Sumtimes, after drinkin, they waller in self-piddy, till you wud think yer Cansir was more'n haff Piskey.

PLANITERRY INFUENZ: These are yer Moon kids, come and go with the tide and wade fer no man. Yer moon's job is to change the water all over the wirld and wen it does it's job (fer quarters) it sure leeves its mark on yer Cansir. Sometimes you can see the hare grown out of ther shoalders.

LOVE: Not too randy a bunch. More passiv, and intens. More intersted in famly feelin. They won't look sideways at ribbled talk, and wen it come to fiscal relations they'd jist as soon back into ther shells, wave ther claws a bit, and even crack-up. Marridge with a Vertgo will side-step yer hole problem.

FAMLY: Cansirs is grate cooks, loves to spred ther bords. As pairints they is somewat overbaring, not wanting ther proganinnies to grow up. Mother Cansir gits histirical wen her son puts on his first long pance or brings home a gurlfrend. (She shud worry more wen he takes off them pance.) Cansir kids is eesly hurt (inside). Like ellafants they never fergit a slite thing. Yer old Cansir kin tell yuh wat he had fer breckfist thirty yeer ago. That's why they kin sit and mope bout wat was dun to them long after it was did. Fer yer Cansir, life is pure shell.

HELTH: Deepends on yer moon, wich controlls yer digestibull organs and yer left eye. (I spose yer rite eye has to fend fer itself.) Cansirs is proan to ulsers, over-wate, swetty foreheds and gastrick disorder. Check yer moon's fase fer how a Cansir kin make out. Yer moon is yer bawdy next to yer sun in yer soler cistern fer its inflooence piddling on erth. It controles berth, brests, and bawdy flooids. Cansirs tenda run outa flooids when yer Moon is outa quarters and not so full. Drink lotsa milk so yer skin won't crack.

LOOKS: Cansirs is sposed to have a crabby look, but don't look at them sideways, makes em nerviss. Face-on they are moon-shape, with stubby nozes, squash feechers, the odd crater, and sometimes a green, cheesy look.

LUCKY STONES: Moon's Tone. Perls. (Yer perls harber in oisters, are best found in months with arse in em.)

FLOWR: Wall-flowr (always lookin' sidewaze).

CULLERS: Off-wite, dull silver, billyus green.

REEDING: Histerical novels.

MUSICK: Yer ballid.

LUCKY DAY: Mundy. (how lucky can you git?)

LUCKY NUMBER: Two. (it's cumpny.)

TENDENCIES: Putting everything on hold.

BEST LOCATION: Covered up with sand.

FAMUS CANSIRS: Leener Horn, yer Stormy Wether girl singer. Saliva Door Dolly, yer Cansir-reelist painter who melts watches on the side. Van Clyburn, the fella who can play with crost hands thru the hole of a musical piece.

KAREERS: Cansirs shud git a stable job, and they cud clean up. They are good workers with big long mamarys and shud mebbe contrack out to Eye Bee Em as compewters.

Is it Your Turn in the Barrel?
Give yourself a rain water treat
with
Butterworth's Balsamic Glycerine Soap

"No more harsh chaps for me." — Gloria Sternend, Walla, Walla, Wash.

"Since Butterworthing myself, my head feels softer than it has ever been."
— P. A. Mckim, Keesterport, N.C.

KEEP IT CLEAN

with Butterworth's

and

You'll Laugh with Delight as You Lather Yourself

Drainpipe Industries

Barrelbottom, Rhode Island

JULY

CHARLIE'S DALY DIAREE

July 1: Dog Daze is here. All of us in heet.

July 2: No wind neether. Cam as the pam of yer hand.

July 3: Son out chasin girls. He'll be no good gittin' in the hay.

July 4: Went to town fer hollyday. It ain't the heet, it's the humanity.

July 5: Make hay wile yer son snores.

July 6: Father-in-law 78 yeer old today. That man takes longer to grow old than anybuddy else I know.

July 7: Son finely got his first kiss. Sez his undyshirt ran up his back like a windowblind.

July 8: Talked to nayber. Says his fat wife has fringe bennyfits. Warmth in winter and shade in summer.

July 9: Sewin' Circle. Buncha wimmen sittin round needlin.

July 10: Quarled with the wife but we ended up a comprymize. I admit I was wrong and she forgive me.

July 11: Tax rebate come back by declaring my stock and chickens as dependents. Every crowd has a silver lining.

July 12: Wrote my accountint, corngrattulated him on bein a Master Rebater.

July 13: Deesided not to go to city with aigs. At 43 cents a doz. it's hardly worth cleenin them off.

July 14: Big dance in our barn. Most poplar reel of all was yer "Pony Trek," three times round the floor then outside fer yer oats.

July 15: Funny thing. Feeld of second timothy behind our barn has bin laid flat.

July 16: Wife wonders why yung girls at dances never seem to git tired. That's cuz they do it in such short shifts.

July 17: Son cot a cold, even tho it's humid. Me I stick to my winter undyware all summer.

July 18: Sunny scool picnic. Son tried to git into the sack event, but won honorable mention fer yer three-legged mens.

July 19. Reel humid. By mid-aftnoon these days I'm droopin like a wax bananner in a modrit oven.

July 20: Hard to work. It ain't the heet, it's the stupidity.

July 21: Wife's cousin come back erly from his hollyday at the Noodist Camp. Sumbuddy spilt hot coffee in his lap.

July 22: Hotted up agin. Wavy lines on rode. Boy Scout helped old lady acrost highway, they both got knocked down.

July 23: Sum smartalec put loaded mouse-trap in my son's swimmin trunks. Now he's allergic to cheese sammitches.

July 24: Wife got so sunburnt her face looks like a wrinkled neecap. I think she likes bein ultry-violated.

July 25: Wanted to treat the wife to ice cream but coodn't git the granny knot outa my hankycheef.

July 26: Anuther wimmin's lunch. I feel run down jist lissening to them doing it to everybuddy else.

July 27: Post-mortars on the lunch. Wife sits on the fone. She shud open a bording house the way she takes in every rumer.

July 28: Frustrated. Tore tellyfone book in haff. Didn't stop wife one bit.

July 29. Still hotter'n a goosed greese poletiss.

July 30: Son sleeps regler. At leest durin the day. At night goes out like a mudcat upriver at sponnin time.

July 31: Still sticky out. Wife won't play the py-anna. She gits so worked up she feels she'll rub all the varnish offa the stool.

THOT FER THIS MUNTH

You can tell yer child is growing up when he stops askin where he come from and starts refusing to tell you where he's going.

YER WIFE SWOP

We joke about the loose morls of everyone in the city, but I never thot sich a thing wood happen round our parts. Oh sure, every yeer bout income tax time, I'm always joshing the wife about the Eternal Revenooers only allowing me $1500 on her fer depreeciation, and that I'm thinking of tradin her in on a second-hand pick-up. But by swinjer, I wouldn't trade the wife fer–well, almost anything.

But I hear tell yer sitty and yer suburb peeple are involved in this kinda round-yer-robins all the time. First I'd ever herd of it was a cuppla yeer ago wen them two base perfessional ballers from the same teem, who'd bin releefin each other on yer mound–started doin' the same thing offa yer mound. And before you cud say Frank Robinson these two fellers traded eech other, spouse, house, the hole kids and kaboodle. I gess they was wat you call in yer ball bizness, wife receivers.

Well, we finely had it happen up our way this summer. We all gang up to git in the hay round our parts–and after we had bailed the lot, we was sittin' round with our wives drinkin beer. Suddenly sumbuddy threw his keys in the middle of the floor, and by golly, we all folleyed soot and before you knew it, everybuddy was divin in hed first, and by hinkus if we all didn't go home in somebuddy else's tractor.

But there was one pare of dubble-yokers got pared off with another pare, ended up in seprit beds and they haven't come apart since. And that was a munth ago, and here's the four of them still pulling the switch on eech other and endin' up in a different set of harness. And so far neether cupple has bothered to git in touch with t'other by phone. But I'll bet you them two wimmen is jist dying to know how them two men is gittin along cookin fer one another.

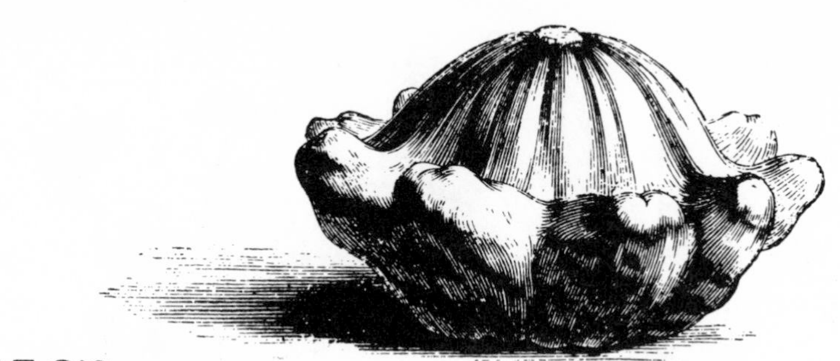

U.F.O'S

I'm talking about yer Unindemnifiable Flying Objecks, not yer United Farmers of Ontario. Myself I've never seen anythin up there out of the way but yer Aroara's Boring Alice, wat they call yer Northern Sites. But there's peeple about has seen strange specks in the sky in broad daylight, wich was still there even after they cleened off ther glasses.

Jist lately more and more peeple clame to have caught site of one of these extry-testial frizzbees from utter space. The first time I seen something winking and blinking out of orbit across the sky was 1958. Turned out to be one of them Roosian Spooknuts with a dog in it, raising his leg at us as he went by circumsizing the Erth.

And I seen on the news once, one of yer Air Farce's spearmintal crafts that looked like a sorcerer, with two fellers sittin' in her testing ther jet repulsions. She had a diafram mebbe twenty feet acrost. So mebbe that's what peeple has bin seein'–a sort of Hoovercraft the shape of a cow-flap.

But by golly, what if it was one of yer spaced-out visiters from another part of yer soler sistern? When you think of all the other blinkers up there in Spiro's Nibble-us, there's no reason some other non-yuman beans couldn't be usin us as a nite-lite. After all, who sez we're the only one in the hole Universel to be inhibited?

Mebbe them specimens is peeking at us fer something to amuse therselves, jist like we do the TV. Mebbe the name of the pogrom they're watching us do here on Erth is yer Wide, Wide, Wide Wirld of Violents.

Now some clames they have met little green Marxians with antenemas sticking out of ther foreheads. Probably more likely Rotarians got up fer a costumed ball. I jist don't bleeve that them inter-planetarium travlers would be foolish enuff to land. I think they hang around Cape Carnivoral wen we send something up like yer Sky Flab becuz they wanta make sure we don't go too far. If we emmygrate over to ther part of the Galexlaxy, then we'll spoil things fer them the way we done alreddy here.

If we try it, its them creechers in the sorcers will start yellin at us: "U! F.O.!"

HELP!

That's the hardist thing to find on a farm nowadays. Used to be you cud hire a man fer fifty dollars a month and bored. That ment everything he cud eat and drink before he cum in the house from the barn. Used to stay out there fer hours pickin at the silo. No more. The hiredman is yer vanishing brood. Wat they call a nacker-on-ism. You can't even rely on yer own issyuh helpin you eether. My boy he don't want to live the life of a crazy gambler and stay here on the farm.

Once in a wile you can git a sitty stranger–fer a short wile–one of them fillosofurs wants to put his back to Nature. We had this yung fella fer two weeks, up and quit becuz he felt he was doin' a teem of mules out of a job. Anuther fella was a forner–had bin mechanical with motors where he come from, but coodn't stand city air. Started to work fer me, but never could git the hang of animals. I showed him how to grab the teets on a cow so's his right hand wood know what his left hand was doing, and he pumped away best part of two hours. Wen I ast him how much milk he'd got, he sed he wasn't sure, coulda told better if ther'd bin a pail under it. I give him a empty pail, he filled it up in about three hours, but as soon as he finished he started giving it back to the cow. He sed she'd got her dirty tail in it, so he thot he'd better run it thru agin.

He finely quit the day he crawled under one of our horses to see why it woodn't go.

YER BIRTHDAY FORTCHUNE AND GUIDE

If you were ever born
JULY 24 up til AUGUST 23
Yer astrological sine is LEEYO
Yer ruling planit is THE SUN

THE YEAR AHEAD FOR ALL LEEYOS: Hold 'em Newt, them Leeyos is heddin' fer the barn! They is always fulla beans and will drop them any-wheres. Last year, you peeple was jist too much, so it's cut-down time on both dreams and expenses. Affairs connected wih the home are favored. Affairs outside the home will git ya into trouble.

LEEYO is yer fixed male on fire, lookin' fer yer Ly-in's share. Bean as how they are born to rool, all they ask is fer to have ther own way in everything. (Some of them seem to work to rool, too.)

Leeyos don't take nuthin' lyin' down, even tho bein' fixed and on fire at the same time must make them feel like a weeny at a roast. They don't like bein' cooped up, and tend to fowl ther own nest, then sumbuddy else has to bring in fresh straw. Life is a jungle, and yer Leeyo wants the run of it.

GOODBITS: Curridge, ambishin, self-rely-ants, diginitty, all yer lyin trates. Good orgy-nizers. As long as you let them be boss of the projeck and never question them, they are good heds in the mane.

BAD BITS: Powr-mad, pompus, conseated, downrite insufferbull.

PLANITERRY INFLUENTS: Jist yer Sun. That's enuff. Sorce of all power, not to menshin spots and freckles. Leeyos love to make it hot fer other peeple. Jist stand up when they cum in a room, hold yer hed in yer hand and you'll be fine.

LOVE: They is pashanut devvils and no misstake. Over-sexed well into senile-titty, they play cat with yer mouse long past other peeple's bedtimes. Jist let them take compleet charge and you'll have a bawl. At the end, don't fergit, they expeck applaws.

MARRIDGE: Yer Leeyo don't take too well to yer State of Holy Acrimony. Avoid a Toreass or a ScorePee-O or yer in fer a baddle roil. And Jiminy kin fool yer Beestly King every time. Cansirs will jist sit back and critisize everything you do. Mebbe Airace or Saggytairass will do, but make sure that yer co-boss don't mind a show-off.

FAMLY: Leeyo is yer father's figger, and tends to dumnate. But they have a pride of kids, and expecks a lot of them, offen fer the wrong reesins. But they have a lotta fun with ther brood, even if the pairint ends up dissa-pointed, and the kids dissa-pated.

LOOKS: A face like a rooler. Hook nose, arch eyebrowse, peerced eyes.

HELTH: Watch yer complection. Leeyos is dry, inflamed, and like as not in heet. This makes them eartable and brings out ther son's spots. Watch yer hart. You are too parshul to rare steak. Eat more pees, plumbs and oringes instedda savaging small animals to deth. And save yer back fer bed.

DRESS: Leeyos like to flash a lot. Plads, stripes, florrid patterns, and when they buy new clothes they tend to see red. When drest they shud not have sich loud clothes neer a hospiddle zone.

LUCKY JOOLS: Rooby, sardonicks, tope-ass.

FLOWRS: Redroze, pawpy, marrygold and peeny.

REEDING: Yer Otta-by-oggerfee. (Ther own, if possbull.)

MUSICK: Grand Opery (Not yer Grand Ole, but that other stuff has no toon, strickly off the A-cuff.)

HOBBYS: Clecting trophees. (Leeyos love to see ther frends git stuffed.)

DAY: Sundy.

LUCKY NUMBER: One. (They're always out fer No. 1)

CULLERS: Redden gold.

TENDENCYS: To git crowned.

BEST PLACES: Outa doors. Rooms don't give em enuff room.

BIG LEEYOSE: George Barnyard Shaw (yer Socialite riter). Mick Jagger (hed of yer Galling Stones). Andy Whorehole (painter fer Camel's soop). May West (erly develper who writ the sloggan: "Go with West, hung man!!")

AUGUST

CHARLIE'S DALY DIAREE

August 1: I'll say this fer summer close. There's no excuse fer marrying a bow-legged girl without knowing it.

August 2: Son's hare looks like the other end of a Gooney bird. Wife ast him if he was bildin a nest.

August 3: Got son's hares cut. Feels he stands out like a hickup at a Baptist picnick.

August 4: Barber had a big day. Three haircuts, four shaves and two hedges.

August 5: Check dogwood tree fer budworms. Ackshully, its bark is worse than its blight.

August 6: Stand in the feelds watchin' girl bikers go by in ther shorts all the way up to yer crost-rodes.

August 7: Too hot to work. Set fer a spell and git porch-broken. Jist watch the traffick and nod like a Sandy Claws in a departmentle store window.

August 8: Son's got his first girl . . . well-to-doer in town. Good match. Her peddygree will reech as far back as my detts.

August 9: Thinkin' of sellin' the old Shev. That meens puttin' the weels back on and movin' them chickens out.

August 10: Wife thinks Shev needs a spray job first. But the chickens has took care of that.

August 11: Son wants to know if he kin keep his town girl in a stile to wich she's acustom. I figger he has enuff money to dress her up to the mornin tub, but not enuff to carry her out into the street.

August 12: Sittin' on my combine, I seen a girl pass with more curves than yer minny-cher golf corse.

August 13: They must pack some of these girls into ther summer dresses by hydrolicks pressure.

August 14: Muggy. Also Tewgy, Weggy, Thurgy and Frygy.

August 15: Dog days. Cat nites fer my son.

August 16: Hot flashes every two minits. Love thunderstorms.

August 17: Wife sez her cousin has got top job as airline ezzecutive. Bet he runs the inside hose in a car-wash.

August 18: The hail, you say. Sounded like a gang of skeltons banging on our tin roof.

August 19: Haven't had a good satisfying crop in five yeer. Reel estate fella sez I should sell it fer a golf corse, let biznessmen come and have a few strokes.

August 20: Git reddy fer fall Chop tree down.

August 21: Wife changes her mind. Wants tree chopped up.

August 22: Bills, bills, bills. The wife says money don't meen nuthin' to her, it jist kinda quiets her nerves.

August 23: Hundred and two in the shade. Don't do me no good. I'm hardly ever in the shade.

August 24: Son wants a ladees watch. The kinda you straps round yer wrist.

August 25: Wife will undergo plastical surgery when I cut off her credit cards.

August 26. These warm nites with yer windows wide open, a TV or phoney-graft turned up loud mite annoy yer nayber. Another good way is to throw a ded cat on his porch.

August 27: Barn dance fer city peeple. Wen I shouted: "Take yer partners" haff them slickers had our girls outside before they knew it.

August 28: Wife has deep tan. It's jist like havin' nicoteen fingers all over.

August 29: Thrashin' about in feelds. Supper after with 8 kinds of pie.

August 30: Musta stufft myself like a outa-work taxidermis.

August 31: Dry today. Throat feels tightern a pair of 98-cent shorts.

THOT FER THIS MUNTH

THE GUVMINT

Wen the guvmint accuses us farmers of being careless with our money, it's a case of yer pot callin yer stummick fat. It's about time they tried to balance ther budge-it and pay ther bills jist like everbuddy else. But no they jist call it yer Nashnul Dett, and keep on past the point wen we'd be too pooped to pay the piper and end up bankruptured.

Mebbe it's time fer the guvmint to take off the velvet glove and give itself the iron finger. If there's gonna be a war on inflammation then let's go the hole hog like we dun durin Wirld War II (that's Wirld War Eleven, accordin to yer Eyetalian numerators). That was wen we had rashin cards, held in our gas, and saved our drippings (Remember them sines: "Ladees don't bring yer Fat Cans in here on Fridays!).

Why shud us poor fokes be the first wave of troops to be in shock in the war aginst the cost of keeping up living? The rich folks is behind the lines sitting on ther holding cumpnies. The cost of livin is gittin so high I think some of us is foolish to pay it. And you can't count on savings no more. That's turned out to be the kind of money that sleeps wile you work. Thrifty has give way to shifty. They used to say a fool and his money is soon parted, but nowadays it's happenin to everybuddy.

Then how does the guvmint git away with it? Estimits. Every guvmint estimit incloods an extry estimit of how much more it's gonna cost than yer ferst estimit. That's how come they always leeve this big deficit on the floor of yer House. And a deficit is what you've got wen you haven't got as much as if you jist had nothin'. If we tried any of this, we'd end up in jail. But the guvmint gits rid of its detts by Nashnullizing them. That's like the alky-holick who solved his problem by poring the booze in all of his bottles into one big container. Himself.

EMLY'S POST

Q. What is manners?
A. The noises you don't make when yer eatin soup.
Q. What is the proper way to dunk a donut?
A. No further than the nuckles.
Q. Wich fingers shud I put in my mouth to whistle for the headwaiter in a French restaurant?
A. Get the fingers out. Insted say: "Garkon Icky!" He'll come over if only outa curiosity.
Q. Wen Sir Walter Rally put his coat on the ground for Queen Lizabeth, why did he do that?
A. So's her back woodn't git dirty.
Q. I'm a teenage boy. What should I do if a girl in my class drops her books.
A. Kick them back to her.
Q. What right has a man to sit on a bus while women are standing?
A. Squatters rights.
Q. A married woman at a party asked if she could sit on my knee. What do I say to her husband?
A. Tell him to stand.
Q. Do young men still open a car door for a young lady?
A. Yes, (a) if the car is new . . . or (b) if the girl is.
Q. Is it proper to pick up a woman in a bar?
A. Well, it sure ain't good manners to leave her lay there on the floor.

EXTRY SENSUAL PRECEPTION

Now I'm not superstishus. Mind you, I'm a dowser. That don't meen I have a bath regler; it meens takin' out yer fork-shape stick until you make water come up. I mind the last time I tried witchin a well, I found oil instead. Them prongs led me right to the spot in the middle of my drivin shed where the crankcase of my car has bin takin' a leek fer yeers.

And there was once I thot I'd seen the devil hisself. The horny old devil come right in our bedroom window and I purt neer blasted him with the BB till my wife cried out it was one of our Holesteens chewin' on the spiorrhea.

But the wife, she puts a lot of stock in her instinks, wat she calls her VIP. One nite she woke me up in the middle of a snore to tell me there was somethin' strange in the room. She had jist watched one of them horrible moovys on the TV like "Dracula Drunk the Bride of Frank'nSteen."

I told her to go to sleep, but she threw off the covers and pointed to these two things down at yer foot of the bed, creepin tord her. I grabbed the old 22. She told this pair of goastal claws to stop comin at her, but they kept on as she drew herself up back agin the backboard. Finely she screemed and told me to shoot at the site. I figgered I'd git a better aim if I turned on the bedlite. Good thing too, or I mighta shot off three or four of the wife's toes. That's what was creepin' up on her.

YER BIRTHDAY FORTCHUNE AND GUIDE

If you were ever born
AUGUST 24 up til SEPTEMBER 23
Yer astrological sine is VERTGO
Yer ruling planit is MURKRY

THE YEAR AHEAD FOR ALL VERTGOS: You finished up last year flat on yer Marse, and now it's time to take a trine toward Venis. Overcome repulsive desires to work all the time. Lie on yer back or even yer stummick, and blow off some steam. Get basic needs out of the way so sumbuddy else kin have the bathroom. But don't peek too erly like you dun last yeer. Try to get up fer Chrismuss.

VERTGO is a dizzy, femnin, erthy sine, altho what's erthy about it is hard to plumb. Vertgo is the sine of yer fussed-budget, the one makes everybuddy else on edge by emptying all the ashtrays and pickin' the lint offa yer coller wile they talk. Funny thing, as they sit ther pickin' ther nits, they offen can't see the trees fer the term-mites. Hard workers tho, even when they try to relacks. They make frends eesly, but then, jist to be helpfull, start pickin' at them fer ther own good, wich it ain't. Mind, yer Vertgo is jist as hard on therself, and takes grate stratusfaction in grabbin falyure oua the jaws of sucksess.

POSTIV UPPERS: Tydy, honist, modess, (Hell, they got lots to be modess about.)

NEGTIV DOWNERS: Worry worts, hype-a-cricketall, fussy and finky.

PLANITERRY INFLEWINCE: If you git a strong Murkry up yer Vertgo's horrorscope, it shows yer intelleckshall's bent. If there's some Leeyo in them they got a better grasp of yer hole-set-up. But if yer Vertgo tends tord yer Libberer, that warms them up and makes them less stand-offish, more lyedownish. Vertgos has fuel fer to burn. It allows them to do what they want, wich is to service as many others as they kin.

LOVE: Bein under the sine of Chastititty kin be a problem if yer simbol-minded. Vertgos is yer orignal Inhibitants. You talk about compleetly aloof, some of them is the compleetest loofs ya ever saw. But where ther's skin ther's fire, and if ya dig yer nails in deep enuff, ya'll find yer Vertgo kin be a sesspool of pashin.

MARRIDGE: Vertgo's love to git tied in martial knots, but by pointin out ther mate's falts, they offen leeve them wimpering under the securety of ther blankits. But Vertgos is deevoted to ther spowses, even tho they may treet them like file-in cabnits. (Love can be neet, but not that way.)

FAMLY: Yer Vertgo pairint ain't too close, offen rools his child by long distants. Oncet in a wile they make a lokel call, and end up doin the kid's homework. Yer Vertgo kid loves scool, and thrives under dissaplin, so is considerd a preevert. They is offen teecher's pets, on accounta they're fasstedious.

LOOKS: High in the forehed, long in the face, dark under yer eye. A cuppla points of interest are nose, chin. (Sharp.)

HELTH: Vertgos is yer happy worriers. They like to keep everythin in mind, incloodin ther deseases, and make great hippy-con-dryacks. They swally vitemin pills like they was Smartys, and are always on a die-yet (nothin' but food and black cawfy). They are rooled by ther nervy sistern, and tend to raze a good crop of hives and ex-enema. Also fond of outbrakes of disinter-dry and dire-rear.

KAREERS: Yer fem Vertgo is the purrfick secktairy. You never git a spot on yer wite coller worker with yer Vertgo. She'll never be had on the carpit fer anything. But they are good in the anal bizness . . . anal-izing . . . anal-alysis . . . anal reports.

LUCKY STONE: Sap Hire.

CULLER: Bloo. All shades. Sep Electrick. (Vertgos don't plug into anything current.)

FAVRIT REEDING: Tex Books.

MUSIC: Old Maladys.

HOBBY: Looking over blooprince.

LUCKY DAY: Whens Day. (Sum day yer blooprince will cum.)

LUCKY NUMBER: 5. (Quince Tupplets.)

TENDENCY: Brown-nosing yer Grindstone.

BEST PLACES: Small towns wher they kin join everythin and be Reecording Seckaterry.

BIG VERTGOS: Greeter Garbo (yer Sweed Reckloose). Gramma Moses (who tuk up paintin and left her boy in front of yer Bull's rushes). Linen Johnson (who wen he was Prescedent made a few dogs pick up ther eers).

DR. FOOTE'S HANDBOOK

"Sunlight in the Nursery"

Public words for private parts.
A vital text for your children

"Calls a spade a garden tool"

Getting yours soon?

W.E.B. FOOTE · · · · SENSABOOKS · · · · PAWTUCKET, RHODE ISLAND

FOUL BREATH????

MILLIONS EXPIRE EVERY SECOND!

Breathing in and out is as natural as life itself. But foulness of breath need not accompany it. It is caused by the decomposing secretions exuded by festering ulcers far back in the head area. Sometimes the membrane covering the bones is eaten away, and sometimes the bones themselves decay.

The sufferer therefrom becomes an object of pity, nay, condescension and revulsion, as the stench from the corroding sores reveals the corruption within. The morbid matter that is swallowed during sleep passes into the wall of the stomach, and enfeebles the digestive process, produces dyspepsia, as well as an excessive secretion of mucus which must perforce by ejected from the nasal passages or alas, snuffed back into the throat. This leads to hawking and spitting of the throat, leaving the nose in heat and dryness, and leading to ringing of both ears. (Stereomucus.) There is a simple remedy for all this. . . . .

SEPTEMBER

CHARLIE'S DALY DIAREE

September 1:	Ninth munth. Laber Day soon.
September 2:	Planted wife's gardin four munth ago. Haven't seen hide ner hare of it since.
September 3:	Shockin corn. Everbuddy agrees.
September 4:	Cut my corn fourteen hour. Any more and you'd have to seprate me from the stubble with a shuvvel.
September 5:	Son still got spring feever. Wife sez love is blind. Mebbe, but it's got a offul keen sense a touch.
September 6:	Smoked bees. Why not? Bin stung every other way.
September 7:	County fair. Wife still gets a lotta attenshun fer her spicy waterdmellin rind.
September 8:	Band consert. Wife kep time with her Adam's apple.
September 9:	Son went to a mind reeder at the fare. She give him his money back.
September 10:	My hare needs cuttin' badly and our lokel barber is the fella to do jist that.
September 11:	Went to barber fer trim and more raunchy storys. Feller like that must have total recoil.
September 12:	Wife sez long skirts is comin back. That's like lockin' yer barn door after yer horse got out.
September 13:	Wife is reeding that book "Yer Exorsesassist" all about the divil gittin busted fer posseshun.
September 14:	Wife took aginst son's new girl on site. Told him to stop kissin short girls or he'd git round-shouldered.
September 15:	New cars comin out this week. Gess that's why ther called Autum-o-biles.

September 16: Ever bin to a house-cooling party? Yung cupple in town tryna brake ther lease on accounta ther seprating.

September 17: Hoorycane and torpedo wether comin. Wind jist blew the cup offa the town pump.

September 18: Must be nice to be flush. Rich town peeple come back from France and installed one of them libidos in ther bathroom.

September 19: Had a dreem I was ridin the train naked. Darn'd if I could find my ticket.

September 20: My own birthdy. Well, yer only old once.

September 21: Wife gimme a party. I was number one plate passer, got a ache in the back of my neck from all that nodding to be plessant.

September 22: Feel like paintin the town and givin her a second coat, but can't find my Dinin' Club Card.

September 23: Got the figgers on son's girlfrend. 32, 28, 36, 54. Last one is her I.Q.

September 24: Fire in the silo. Volunteer briggade rushed out, damped it down then rushed back to fire hall before they forgot wich soot was trumps.

September 25: Smartalec son come home from scool, says human body is 92 persent water and not worth much. Jist wish he'd do something with that other 8 persent.

September 26: Hit on hed by two by twice. Got giddy there fer a haffa minit. It was almost worth it.

September 27: Leeves start to fall, speshully wen my old truck backfires.

September 28: News in town is that the Mare's wife come home from her holyday in Ittly, pinched but happy.

September 29: Indians start havin ther summer. Gits hottern a Quebeck heeter.

September 30: Car collusion. Why do I run into accidents that start out to happen to somebuddy else?

THOT FER THIS MUNTH

FALL FAIR

If you want to git a darn good peece of razzberry pie, (and they don't care how much butter you put on it) you can't beat yer avridge Fall Fair.

Now don't expeck no harem-scarem girls boomping ther daisy, and you won't see no freek-out neether–none of that Jo-Jo the dog-face woman walks, talks and crawls on her belly like a reptile. One yeer I mind they had a beerded lady, but next yeer she dun a depillertory ad on the TV and we ain't seen hide ner nair of her since. My favrit was always Britannica, the Yuman Cyclepeedierast. She was tattooed from hed to foot, and on her belly was the Grate Colorado Train Wreck of 1919 wich she would re-enact fer twenty-five cents by moving her abominable mussles.

I never cared too much fer the Dubble-Hedded boy from Borneo. He was a fake. Oh, he had the two heads all right but I don't bleeve he was from Borneo at all; looked more like a cuppla fellers I used to go to school with in Parry Sound. Last yeer they tried havin a flee circus as part of the middle-way but our dog walked off with the show.

There'll be a Murry-go-Round and a Ferrous Wheel but no Rolly Coaster. But if you want to see what a horse looks like, there's two shows, yer light draft on the one day, and yer hevvy draft on the hevvy day, jist like in the ladies' ads. They say a horse show is jist a buncha horses showing ther asses to a buncha horses asses showin ther horses. But if you haven't bin atall, you otta go agin.

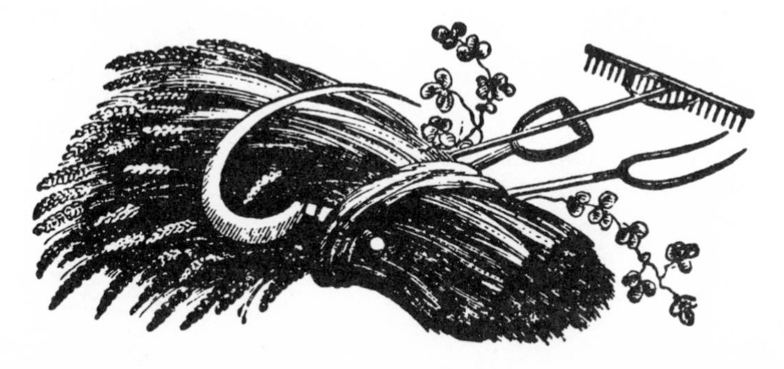

ADULTERATED EDICATION

As a D.O.P.E. (Doctor of Persnal Experience) I feel like a post-granulate in the school of life, but the wife feels that I'm an old dog who kin still turn a few tricks. This fall she is tryna sine me up in one of them nite school corses. She has enrolled herself up in both Pianna Tunin and Shorthand. Both of wich will come in handy wen she gits the hang of them, fer I'm always short-handed wen it comes to tightening up barb-wire fences.

She thot I shood take a corse in Human Relations, but my gol, we got enuff of those. And everyone of them expecks a present at Chrismuss. I'd ruther take up Gynological Studdys. That's tracing back yer Incesters till you come up aginst a horse theef. But the fella in charge at the Commune-a-titty College, yer Cash Registrar, he wants to pick a corse for me. He thinks I shood git in on a practickle demonstration of Animal Husbandry. I don't know how to tell him this, but I once fired our hired man fer tryin' that in the barn.

WOMEN HAVE DOG DAYS TOO!

Overcome the Fatigue of Shopping with a cup of

The Laxative Tea that picks you up and lets you off the hook gently.

Try the virtues of tannic acid combined with the vegetable extract to relieve chronic weakness, induration, retroversion, bearing down, suppressed or painful periods, and all perversions incident to life change.

Also Stimulates the Hair Bulbs and Prevents Loss of Color in the Tubes!

Sent by mail on receipt of price

Dr. Piercin's Female Remedies, Sick River Junction, Mich.

YER BIRTHDAY FORTCHUNE AND GUIDE

If you were ever born
SEPTEMBER 24 up til OCTOBER 23
Yer astrological sine is LIBBERER
Yer ruling planit is VEENIS

THE YEAR AHEAD FOR ALL LIBBERANS: Check yer burnt-out fuses from last year. Once yer box is in order agin, find somebody else to take care of the charges. Let somebody else paddle yer stern in life's canoe. This yeer is gonna be a zinger, but don't go to ex-streams to prove it. Big investmints ahed. Mostly in yer own helth, if yer smart.

LIBBERER is another of yer Carnal sines, rooled (and fooled) by Veenis. But some Libberers is well-ballantsed, on accounta ther simble is yer Scales. That's why they all weigh one thing aginst another, but kin no more make up ther minds than my boy his bed, on accounta they allways see both sides. It leeves them cot on the horns of a dillenemna.

Libberans is always saying to sumbuddy else: "It's not rite, it's not fare!!" as if they was talking about Moehamid Alley's left foot. But it's eesy to git them to change ther minds, because they wanta git on the good side of ever-buddy, and are always tryin to be all things t'all men. They was born with the sine "On Approoval" and will do anything to git it, even if it meens changin ther pinions more offen than ther undywares.

POSSITIVS: Charmin, eezy goin, sweet and refind. An esthetick tipe.

NEGGITIVS: Flirty, frivluss, resentfull, and pritty umbalanced.

PLANITERRY INFLOONCE: It's Veenis gives Libberer yer perpetchyal emotion. Sometimes they swings both ways, jist to even things out.

LOVE: Libberers feel harddun by if ther stable mate don't allow fer yer give and yer take. Mind you, it's yer Libberer expecks to be give to while ther on the take. This is yer Airy sine and not too Erthbound about love. Mebbe they shud try it in a Helluva-copper! Romantickle Libberers will best snuggle in front of a roaring Fire sine like Leeyo. They don't like it pushy or brashy wile ther serching fer bewdy. They don't like it wen yer Airace cums on strong in a red satin nighty with "Come On Big Boy!" writ all over the frunt.

FAMILY: Wimmen Libberers, and even men, make plezzant pairints, spend a lot on ther kids, and treet them soft as icecreme. They pertend to be DissplinaryAryans but the threts is mostly wind, and yer kids soon gits to know wich way yer wind blows. Yer Libberer child lerns to be a Dipple-mat, a regler Kissassinger.

HELTH: Jist becuz yer lucky in love, Libberer, don't mean ther ain't gonna be plenty of trubble below the belt. Stay away frum white suger in yer sweet and refined way, eat strawburys insted fer to git high on yer minral salts. Watch yer kidnees, and ware long flannel drores wen yer feeling out of shorts.

LOOKS: A lotta Libs is lushus lookers. You take yer Brigate Bardough and that Catrin DeNerve. I'd take her even without Channel Nummer Five. Libberers don't like to be aloan, and rarely gits the chants. They kin rap ther boss round ther little finger, and sumtimes so permamint that that finger ends up with a famillyer ring on it.

KAREERS: Libbers don't like to do the dirty work. Scraping bottoms of yer barls is not fer them. They is too high-strung-up. Better they shud be fashin moddles, bewtitians, or infeerior desecraters. Libberers avoid discords, and make better dipple-mattresses than peeano tooners. Also ther high-stringiness makes them regler swingers on a trap-ease, and with all that balance, gud bankers or even a cirkus jugular.

LUCKY STONE: Oaple. (It's a millstone fer everbuddy else.) Also yer semmy-preshustones, corl and burl. (Corl is small sea animals got crusty and give up.)

FLOWRS: Dazey, vilit, focksgluv, and golding rod. (Reed "Graze Allergy in a County Churchyard.")

CULLERS: Wite, yella, pastill blue.

FAVRIT READING: Poetree or even verse.

MUSIC: Lite opera. (Not too hevvy, like mebbe six bars from yer Choclit Soldyer.)

HOBBY: Bein' pritty.

LUCKY NUMBER: Six. (six appeels.)

TENDENCY: To git even.

BEST PLACES: Crowds.

FAMOUS LIBBERS: France List (yer classick oppstar, the Libber-otchy of his day). Sairy Burnhart (yer old french stage-coach). Pee-Air Truedough (yer Primed Minster of Canda). Evil Kineevil (yer moter-cycled dare-Divvil went off by hisself over yer Snake Livver Cannon but ended up muffing his dive).

LIGHT IN DARK CORNERS...

WHY NOT MAKE SEX A SCIENCE?

This clever little book is a Guide to the Purity of Physical Mad and Maidenhood. Written for those intending to marry, Or those not doing too well so far.

Teaches the philosophy of Generation and the Possible Derangements between Men and Women. Special Chapter on the Disadvantages of Celibacy. Abuses and Disabuses.

Common Sense in the Nursery . . . talking familiarly with Would-be Mothers before and after.

How Parents Can Control; the Sex of their Child. (up to the age of sixteen)

Perpetuating the Honeymoon without Stimulants.

Child Labor. False or True? How to Make it Without the Doctor. Planning for the Changes Ahead (What to do with the Father after the Baby Comes . . . Triangular Relations).

FIVE FOOT SHELF Bookco. Five Foot, Wisconsin.

CHARLIE'S DALY DIAREE

October 1: Work's all dun this fall. I feel jist as lazy as a dressmaker's husbind.

October 2: Fist fite in Macdonald House Hotel, over yer United Nations. Probly the only time a U.N. matter ever reely got settled.

October 3: Need a good-sized rake fer my leeves, but the son is in town.

October 4: Clip stubble, go to church.

October 5: Time fer nutting yer acorns, but not yer spring lambs.

October 6: Wife tuk me to consert of atone-all musick. I gess it's us is sposed to a-tone fer it.

October 7: Hoping somebuddy will cum soon and squeeze my apples.

October 8: Took nine yeer-old neece to a good square dance. She's gettin ahed by leeps and bounds.

October 9: Wife tells our son to go out and cut some kindling. Laff, I thot he'd split.

October 10: He did too. Up the lane heddin fer town.

October 11: Seven yeer cycle is finished. Wile ridin it, our son hit mail box.

October 12: Somebuddy's weddin anniversery. The wife thinks it was the day Prince Raindeer made a Prinsess outa Gene Kelly.

October 13: Box social. Ate the wife's of corse.

October 14: Found old elm tree in town wher I carved wife's inishuls thirty-five yeer ago. Cop come up and fined me fifty dollars fer defacing pubic property.

October 15: Wife ran into old frends. First fifty dollars deduckable.

October 16: Family re-union. Watering our roots.

October 17: Had pitcher took beside my third cousin who is big in Cleeve-land. I look like her calf.

October 18: Wife's sister stayin with us. First time I saw her I took aginst her on site.

October 19: Wife's sister clames she has never let a harsh word pass her lips. That's becuz she talks thru her nose.

October 20: Asked brother-in-law why he got married. He kin tell me wen and where, but danged if he kin remember the why part.

October 21: Met a distant cousin has a handshake should only be used as a toornikay.

October 22: Famly party agin. Wife backed into a tray of hore dovers, took four of us two hours to pick the olives out of her.

October 23: Brother-in-law and his wife is trying to make a go of ther maridge fer the sake of the home movees.

October 24: Met a little neece I used to bounce on my knee. If I tried it now she'd bounce me on my hed.

October 25: Famly fite. Brother-in-law got drunk, struck his wife and she fainted. Fainted with her left, cracked him with her ring-finger left.

October 26: Beat visiting cousin's overnite bag senseless when she herd a rattlesnake inside it. Turned out she had left on her lectric toothbrush.

October 27: Wife thinks I need a new swetter. Hard to git parts. She nit the last one frum a '52 Volkswagon.

October 28: Turned cold. Didn't dress fer it. Shivvering now like the fender on a flivver.

October 29: Sure feel the frost on my punkins.

October 30: Hollerwean. Can't tell wether them teenyagers is in costoom or not. Wife won first prize eetin a apple thru a tennis rackit.

October 31: Shud have ankered our outbildins. Young fry turned a few tricks.

THOT FER THIS MUNTH

Money can't buy friends. But it sure helps you rent some.

YER DIRTY THIRTIES

The only way to save money these days is to have good helth and a poor appytite. Mind you, money isn't everything. Sometimes it ain't even enuff. But it does keep you in touch with yer children.

But there are some things money can't buy. Mind you, it USED to buy them. You take wen I was yung back in the thirties there was a shortedge of cold cash. That's becuz nobody could hold on to it fer long enuff to keep it warm. We was all divided into two groops–them as was too poor to buy meat, and them as was too rich to digest it.

Posterity was jist around the corner, they kept sayin, but it sure staid there. But man does not live by bredlines alone. In some ways peeple in them days was a lot happier with next to nuthin than they are today with ther nose agin yer Tiffnee glass tryna see wat they kin buy with ther creditable cards.

Today not many peeple do the kind of work wher you have to scrape yer boots before you comes in the kitchen. It sure helps to have bin poor wen a recession comes along, becuz peeple with money to burn in 1929 was the first to meet ther match. Ther the ones jumped offa high bildins to a deffinit conclusion. The rest of us jist ground our teeth, and them as had none, ground ther gums.

Now as far as yer present recession is concerned, the guvmint keeps tellin us we're outa the woods. That meens we're up the crick. But a recession jist meens that everybuddy has to live the way I always have. And the guvmint will think up something to git us out. Last time it was Wirld War II.

But I dunno why they called it "Yer Dirty Thirties." The only smut I ever seen in them days was on the wheat.

ARE YOU A TRICK OR A TREET?

I don't know if you city peeple still go out holloweenying. Up our way we celibate with a big party where we all git up like a fancy-drest ball. Used to be we'd go out soaping winders and pushin' over the odd outhouse, but that's offul hard to do now with them indore skeptical tanks.

This yeer Valeda (that's the wife and former sweethart) wants me to get myself up as a moose. She wants to put a hatrack on my hed and drape me over the fender of the car. I told her it mite put the frost on my punkins.

She's jist tryna git back at me fer last year, wen we took off the parts of Elmer and Elsie, yer Bordon cow and bull. We rented these hairy soots with hooves and a tale, and a horny part in front, and put 'em on before we drove over to this party on the next consession hard by the town line.

I was drivin' with my bull's hed on and din't see too well thru the slits. Mebbe that's why I didn't notice whatever it was in the rode that gimme a flat tire. Wen we got out to fix it, I reelized I had left my jack off in the drivin shed too. That's why the wife had to hold up the Stewedbaker wile I loosened yer nuts on the tire.

Well sir, we was jist in the middle of all this, when the wife purt near drop the car on my foot. Standin' starin' at us not five rod away was a grate big Herfert bull with a ring in his nose, pawing the ground with his hoof, and his both nostrils die-latin' like elevater doors. He looked like he was loded fer bear, or anything else he could find to get ingaged to. He cud cleer that snake fence any time he'd a mind to. And bleeve me, the way he snorted, he sure had a mind to.

The wife looked at me and sed: "Charlie, he's comin' over. What's that animal gonna do?" I said: "Valeda, the thing to decide is what we're gonna do. Now if he jumps over that fence, me, I'm gonna git down on all floors and pertend to eat grass. As fer you, you'd better brace yerself."

Life Size Doll on Request.

This doll is an exact replica of an old hand-painted French model. She will live in your memory long after childhood days have passed.

Rosy cheeks, golden hair, indestructible head.

Optional equipment; gold-plated beauty pin, red stockings, high heeled shoes and face veil. Height 5′6″. *Can wear your wife's cast-off clothing with ease.*

TRANS-VESTRY APPLIANCES DOLLSVILLE, TEXAS.

YER BIRTHDAY FORTCHUNE AND GUIDE

If you were ever born
OCTOBER 24 up til NOVEMBER 22
Yer astrological sine is SCOREPEE-O
Yer ruling planit is MARS

THE YEAR AHEAD FOR ALL SCOREPEEONS: You've had yer peeriod of quiet, and if you haven't missed the other kind, this is yer year to howl, and mebee bite a bit too. Yer retrogrades is behind you, so rise above yer trifles and try not to go thru the changes wen the Moon gives no quarter. Try to avoid bizness affairs between 9 and 5.

SCORPIO is the sine marked "Danjer" . . . rooled by Mars . . . a fixed sine but with a sting in its endtails. Scorepeons live intents . . . they do nuthin' by halfs and kin be offal cut-ups . . . they have grate pursnal maggotism, but it's like settin' nex to a Vulcanoe fulla moultin' larva. Some of them is sad-ole-massakists . . . do a lotta crool work . . . some scorin' agin them as has crost them, others saving ther best stings fer therselves. Yer Scorepeeon is the only noan critter kin kill itself with its own stinger. Wen I tell ya it's a fixed sine, I'm not kiddin'. Scorpeeos got all the fixins.

POSSETIV POINTS: Determined, suttle, pursistent, loil, ardint, pashnit and fulla purpiss.

NEGGYTIV BARBS: Jellus, stubbern, seecretiv, suspishus and sadipstick. A reel stinger, the pits of yer Sodyack.

PLANITERRY INFLOONCES: Pluto, that dog, is Lord of yer Underwhirld, and that makes Scorpeeos wat have not bin house-trained, a bit sneeky, leeky, creepy, slipry, stelthy and oily. Mind, all these here trates kin be turned to gud if ya git a job with yer C.I. of A.

LOVE: What is this sting called? Love? More like strait sex. Sex is yer over-drive of yer ScorerP.O. It's not that they is so darn good at it, but ever-buddy else is so meedy-ochre. If love makes the wirld go round these hellers is in the driver's seet. Ther so all-fired keen on it, they sumtimes skeer ther partners away. But yer ScoredPeeO better channle his strenth, and not do it all the time, fer they face enuff upsin downs as it is.

FAMLY: Score Peeos is determind ther kin will suckseed cum helen high-water. They makes feerful pairints . . . severe and stubbern . . . plenty of Gumfites at yer Not-so-Okay Corale. Home life is never dull wat with missals and crockery flyin' thru the jinration gap.

LOOKS: Dark'n swarty, heavy browse, bull-dogged chins.

HELTH: Score Peeos is good medicle stewdents, and look after therselves. But watch out fer yer more sociable diseases . . . gunner-rear and all that kinda clap.

KAREERS: Ther's nothin' trivvy-a about yer Score-Peeon. They wanta dig down to yer roots, wether it's die-section or grave-diggin. Also make good path-logicalists, sick-eye-atrists, sewer operaters, and mentle detectivs. They work hard and wen it cums to dissaplin they are all regler whips.

LUCKY STONE: Toepaths.

FLOWRS: Honey Suck-ill.

FAVRIT CULLER: Dryed blud.

FAVRIT REEDING: Ackshun tails. (Dock Savidge, James Blond—but they'd ruther do than reed, cuz they genrully know wher th'ackshun is.)

FAVRIT HOBBY: Clecting scalps.

MUSICK: Marshal.

LUCKY DAY: Choosedy.

LUCKY NUMBER: Ate.

TENDENCY: Lookin' fer a good piece of mind.

BEST PLACE: Neer water. (Helps to die-loot ther persnality.)

BIG STINGERS: Martin Loofer (not him as was king, but him as was Protestant agin yer Pope in his Middle Ages). Matted Hairy (yer Wirld Whore number one spy). Dusty Evsky (yer undyground Roosian rit about "Crimea and Punishmint") Joe Knee Mitchell (yer young fokes singer). George Gallup (well-known Pole).

NOVEMBER

CHARLIE'S DALY DIAREE

November 1: Coal? Oil? Yer burning question.

November 2: Brooding time fer both chickens and us.

November 3: Lime phosphate fer the chickens. It's on the house.

November 4: Son so sleepy at morning chores he fell down and stomped on hisself.

November 5: TV is broke. We tride to amuse ourselfs by hidin behind the furnicher.

November 6: Wife's cousin got good job with post-office. He stands behind a window all day and sez "this one's closed, try the next one."

November 7: TV still broke. We haven't even got the re-runs.

November 8: Yes, we have no Bonanza.

November 9: Wife is sittin' there in livid culler.

November 10: Wife's sister's birthday. I give her a step-ladder with matchin squeegee.

November 11: My brother-in-law foned, told me he has one month to live. That's how long his wife is plannin on stayin with us.

November 12: Wife and sister settin at supper told eech other everythin they knew, and still went on talkin.

November 13: Wife's sister called me a male shovinist pig. Th-th-th-that's all folks!

November 14. Wife wants to join Wimmen's Librium. I think equality with me is gonna be an offal step down for her.

November 15: When I shout, the wife and her sister jump. All over me.

November 16: I still ware the pants in this house. You kin see them under the apron.

November 17: Wife's sister sat at pyanna and sang poplar songs. At least they was before she sung them.

November 18: TV fixed. Mebbe if I call the vet we can git the wife's sister dun too.

November 19: Went to docter. He told me avoid excitemint, don't kiss any wimmen except the wife.

November 20: Saw Miss Amurka contest on TV. Must lern to be content with wat the wife ain't got.

November 21: Marridge is a fifty-fifty preposition, but the wife and her her sister say they don't understand frackshuns.

November 22: Went to a dance. They had a five peece band. Darn shame they couldn't lern more.

November 23: Wife's sister in bad mood. Must have got up on wrong side of floor.

November 24. Wife and sister staid up fer Late, Late Show, "The Thing that Ate Boston". They got up fer National Antrim, and wife sat down on her knittin' needles.

November 25: Wife to hospiddle in ambullience which dubbles as a herse and strained her back bracing her feet agin a coffin.

November 26: Wife now lying in hospiddle under the doctor's soopervisor.

November 27: Wife's sister gone home. Went out and got tighter'n a bull's arse in fly time.

November 28: Woke up with tung too large to fit inside my mouth.

November 29: Wife operated on fer 34 stitches and 2 needles.

November 30: Wife up and walkin around without a stitch.

THOT FER THIS MUNTH

If yer TV is broke, reed a book. They don't have wavy lines, snowstorms, or pauses fer commershuls.

THE RIGGERS OF MORTIS

This is a bad enuff munth anyways, without it bein the time wen Father Times takes his sythe and starts cuttin us down in windrows and puttin us away fer seed.

I've jist come back from the layin-in of a secund cousin over to Coldwater. He packed it in at 79, just missin' being one of yer ock-toe-gin-Aryans. But considrin what's comin' up on the world's bullet-in bored, I don't think he missed much.

The wife didn't go because she don't have relations in Coldwater now. But she was sprised when she herd. "Why, Charles," she sez, "I didn't even reelize old Ivan had passed away!"

"My gol, Valeda," I sed, "he better have. I don't think us four pole-bearers was jist rehearsin with him!"

Mind you, the wife don't bleeve in deth. She even put a sine on her own father's grave: "He is not ded, he only sleepeth." I haven't the hart to tell her that she and her father ain't foolin' nobuddy but therselves with that sleepin' stuff.

She's bin high on creamy-toriums ever since one of her kin got burned in the funeral bizness down in the city. Valeda figgers it's a good thing fer me on accounta ther's not enuff room in the family mussle-linoleum. She thinks all men shud be cremated equal, and plans to put my ashes in a aig-timer so I'll go on workin fer her after I'm gone.

But she herself wants to go the way of wages and prices. She wants to be froze. There's this outfit, the Cry-onyx peeple, who puts you in a state of suspended constipation like a side of beef, until they find a cure fer wat ails you. Then they raze yer tempacher sevral degrees Fattenheat, defrost you and bring you back to compost mentis.

And till that time, there you are stiff and froze, lyin' in a glass case with yer name on it, jist like Baskin' Robins ice creem.

The only thing worries the wife about this set-up is if I survive her. She don't want me comin' in and standin' in front of her in the deep freeze and sayin: "Thar she lays, jist as she was in life."

INSURENCE

I dunno why the Insurence salesmen start to come out of the woodwork this time of yeer. But they turn up jist as regler as the bugs in the wallpaper of the spare room wen we turn on the Que-beck heeter.

First comes yer Lifer feller tellin me to come to terms with my own end. He tells me I shud pervide fer the wife, becuz at age 85 there are 7 wimmen for every man. It's a actuary fact. But who cares about them statisticleticks? At age 85 it's too late fer a man to be around 7 wimmen.

Besides the wife she don't want me to take out life insurence. She wants fire insurence as she plans to have me go up in smoke wen I meet my Cremator.

So we settled fer the fire insurence, becuz you never know wen somebuddy will start arson around. That agent tried to sell me tornadoe insurance too but I told him I didn't know how to start a tornadoe.

He laffed, until I ast him how much I'd get if my barn burned down tonight. He sed: "Probly ten yeers."

THANKSGIVING

The first founderers of yer Boston States was a buncha Puritanicals called yer Prodigal Fathers. You kin reed about them in a book by John Bunny called Yer Pills Grim Progress. They dropped off a buncha Plymuth Rocks and started to lay in ther settlement. But it was the wrong time of yeer, jist past harvest, and nobuddy had time to spill his seed on the ground.

But they got by thanks to yer bounty of yer Injin, who taught them how to grouse a bit thru the winter, and make punkin pie. It was later that them Puritains returned the favor by puttin' the bounty on yer Injin. Fer they had come over here so they cud worship God as they seen fit. And after they got here, they tried to git everybuddy else to purify God in the same way, and if you didnt do it ther way, you got ducked in a pond till you didn't know witch end was up.

But, anyway, the upshat of the hole rang-dang-doo was the invenshun of Punkin pie out of an old Injin game called Squarsh. So keep yer fork after you polish off that turkey's jibberlets.

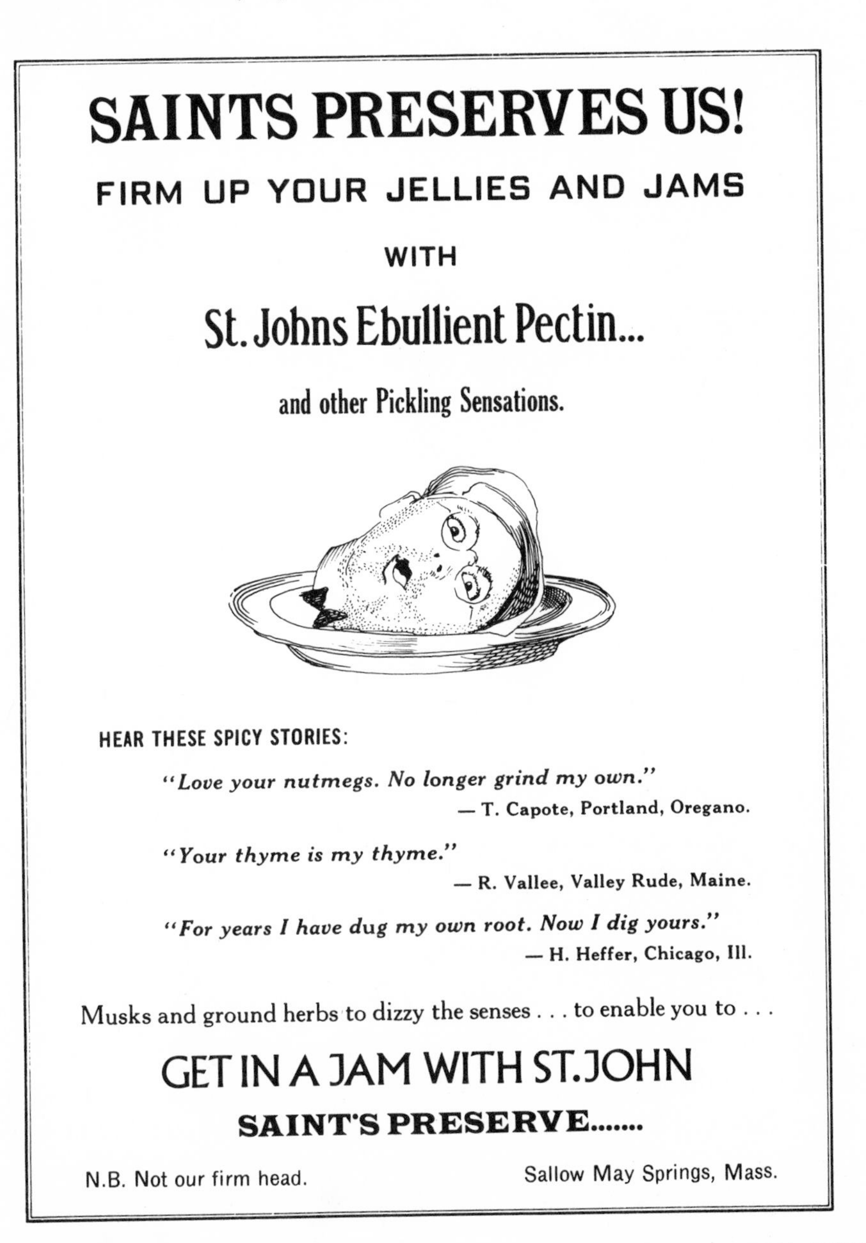

YER BIRTHDAY FORTCHUNE AND GUIDE

If you were ever born
NOVEMBER 23 up til DECEMBER 21
Yer astrological sine is SAGGYTAIRASS
Yer ruling planit is CRAPPYCORN

THE YEAR AHEAD FOR ALL SAGGYTAIRASSES: Alright, you bragged all last year. It's time to cleen off the faery dust frum yer feet, dry out yer dreems, and keep yer feats paralell to the ground. This yeer, stay home and impress yerself insted. Take yer pleasures one at a time and avoid exposure. And fer crynoutloud, let yer impulses sway in the cam, cool breeze of non-attachmint.

SAGGYTAIRASS is yer by-sectional figger, borne out of yer Geek mith (That's a ferry story fer the simble-minded, and tells how some God gotoffa his Mount Olimpuss, disguyzed hisself in his beestliness, and merged with a yuman bean. This mixed marridge led to the patter of clove-in hooves, and brot forth yer Sentor . . . front end is a fella with a bow and arrer, and the rest has the bawdy of a quadra-ped). That's why ther called Sentors, jist like Warshinton, because up front they is arch and aims to please, but they end up as a horse's ass.

And that's yer Saggytairass–a big pointer lookin' fer a tar-git with a peece of tale behind. A mixed blessing. That's why they prants around restless and sumtimes gallup off reckless in all dreckshuns. Saggy's is the freebies of yer Sodyack . . . they don't like to be broke or fensed in or tyed down. They like furaway feelds. That's why it's so hard to git them down the neerest bridle path.

FISCAL FEECHERS: Long strait Geek nose, pointy chins, archy eye-brows awmund eyes, well-shaped hed (sum more like a septic tank) and fair curly hair most places.

POSSTIVE ASSPICKS: Versytile, sinsear, dependibble, fillisofficle, and an open mind at both ends.

NEGGTIVS: Cairless, tackless, and give-in to exaggregation. Boystruss, they act out of their hed, on the sperm of the momint.

PLANITERRY OVERHANG: Moniturd by Joopter, which is the largest bit of gas in any constipation in yer soler's sistern. This makes yer Saggytairyan expansive to deel with. Also harty, cheerfull, and broad minded . . . (will follow them anywares). Cheerful to the point of noshusness, optimistick, and born gamblurs, alwaze reddy to go fer craps.

HELTH: Saggytairasses are long or loose livers. They need a canter for to exorsize their hipps'n thize. It's good fer them to have the weakly trots. I dunno witch doctor said it, but dandylion wine cleers ther your-a-nary passidges, and moss eezes ther inflammation. (I'm not sure wher you put the moss if yer a Rolling Stone, but these daze inflammation seems to be hittin' everbuddy.)

LOVE: Yer horsey set is outstanding in his feeld and the life of the party, but don't care to be sadilled with the same rider fer too long. This mounts to sum problems, fer yer Saggytairasses idee of marridge is to stall and stall till they bin thru the hole herd.

MARRIDGE: The mare the merrier is Sag's ideel. Stay away from Vertgos and Piskeys or you'll get a lotta yer tale cut off. Try Libberer or Aquah-hairyanns insted.

KAREER: They got wat counts, these sure-foot four-foots. Not talint. Luck. Yer Saggytairass is sure of the hole wirld's sucksess. As long as they kin void rooteen and find sumthing keeps ther mind offa ther work, the world will be ther ball and they'll bounce all over it. They make gud explorers . . . jockeys (nag not disc) Vetnairy-Aryans, and horse trayners (flat, steeple, or even with a sulky behind).

LUCKY ROCK: Turkwas.

FLOWR: Tarnation.

CULLER: Purpull.

FAVRIT REEDING: Racy storys.

MUSICK: Nashnill Anthems. (also Nashvill)

HOBBY: Window dressing. (Kin expose you to trubble with the pleece.)

LUCKY DAY: Thirsdy.

LUCKY NUMBERS: Three. (doesn't say wich three)

TENDENCYS: Bluntniss. (this is sumtimes not too sharp.)

BEST PLACES: Over the hills and fire-away.

FAMOUS SAGGASSAS: Frank Sinotta (a cruner with old booby sockers); Winsom Churchle (the one during the war give everybuddy two finger up); Red Fox (on that junkman's TV show); Sammy Davis, (the last of the Red Hot Mau-Maus).

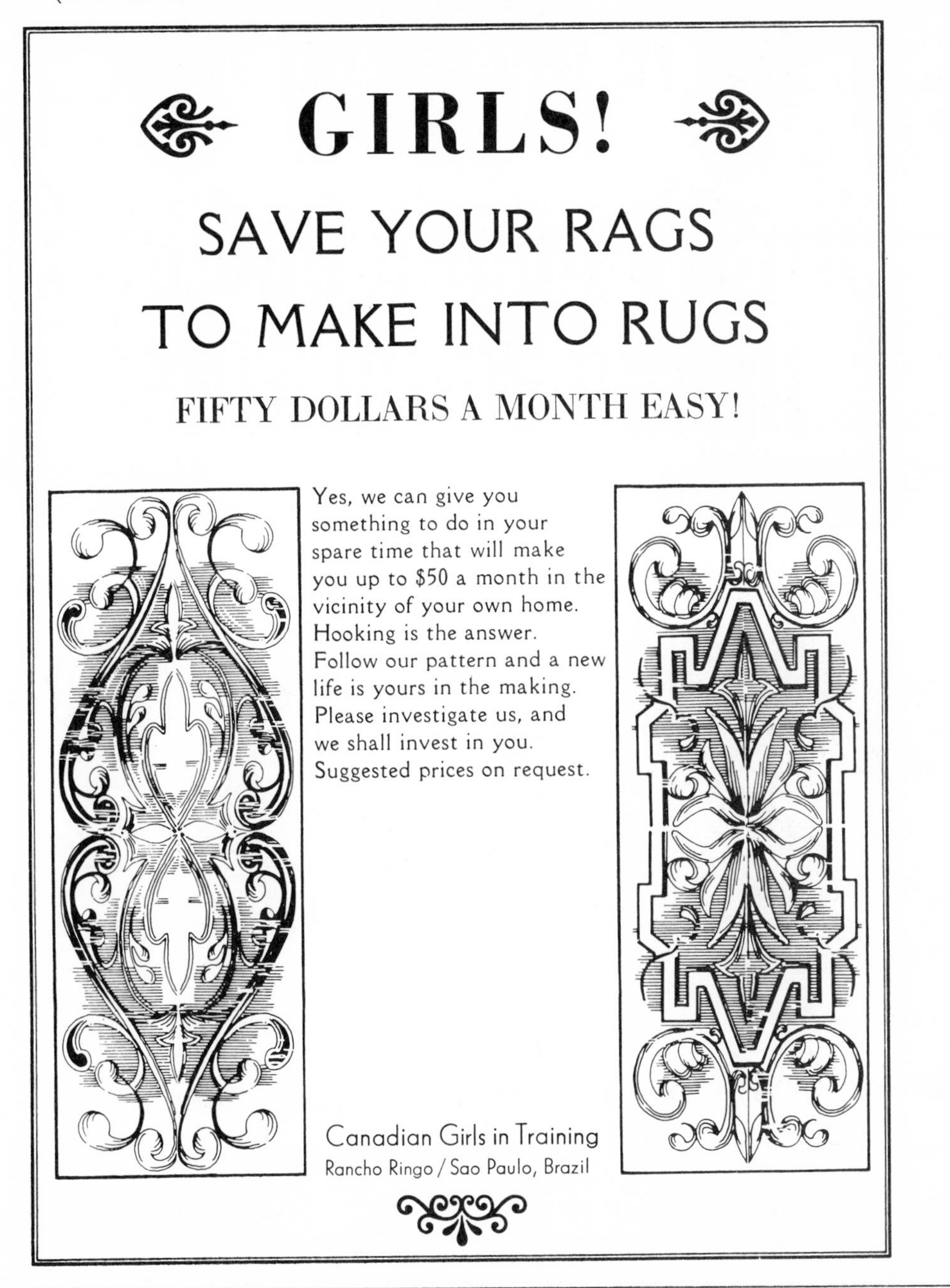

AT LAST! AT LAST!

Stomach Seat or Pin Worms Dosed Off!

Pelvic Drains and Offensive Discharges
Our Specialty.

Get in the Swim with

Hirst's Hoarhound and Indian Worm Killer

"We will Worm our way into your hearts."

RELIABLE EXTERMINATORS (Internal Division) Silverfish Lane, Bridgeport Conn.

DECEMBER

CHARLIE'S DALY DIAREE

Dec. 1: Frusterated. Thot of goin to one of them massadge parlers. Everyone likes to feel kneaded.

Dec. 2: Watched Wirld War II on Late Show starrin John Wain.

Dec. 3: Wife's sister wen she got home threw out a vozz with her husband's ashes in it. From now on he'll use a ashtray.

Dec. 4: Wife comin' home tomorra. This old hawg'll be rootin' fer her.

Dec. 5: Treeted wife to pine-apple Sundy in town. High stool. Had trubble gittin up. Wen girl sed "Crushed nuts?" I told her it was roomatizm.

Dec. 6: Yep. This is the time of yeer we feel old age creaking on us.

Dec. 7: Perl Harber's Day. And I know how it musta felt. Son cum home from scool with a buncha Zeroes.

Dec. 8: Son wants to take Karotty lessens. Figgers on makin' money on the side splittin' kindlin.

Dec. 9: Was attacked in shower by 2 black widda spiders wile eyes fulla sope. Bashed them ded with scrub-brush. Turned out to be wife's falsie eyelashes.

Dec. 10: Winter draws in. Winters drawrs on.

Dec. 11: I'm startin to curl up at the edges and show sines of frost.

Dec. 12: Watched TV. Sumtimes it's better to close yer eyes and pertend it's raddio. Whatever happen to slides?

Dec. 13: Son brung his girl out and showed her a groundhog. She expected to see pork sossidge.

Dec. 14: Wife bored. Wants to live in the city where the evenin papers come on the streets afore noon.

Dec. 15: Son wants to go to city too. Enrole in a trade scool called yer Disco Tech.

Dec. 16: Who wants to live in a condom minimum?

Dec. 17: Told the wife her hair is startin to match her eyes. The white parts.

Dec. 18: Wife got mad, went out into barnyard to giv a hen a rinse.

Dec. 19: Good time last nite jist thinkin bout the ole days. Haven't laffed so much since the wife's sister fell offa the drivin shed and laid her scalp open.

Dec. 20: Bin countin up. Find I have six frends. Jist enuff to carry me out thru that parler and into the ground.

Dec. 21: Cleened up attick. Wife workin on a patchwork quilt made outa 1748 men's ties.

Dec. 22: Post office has rush. Dubbled the staff. One fer sittin and sortin, the t'other fer standin and handlin.

Dec. 23: Church Consert. Wife sung thru the hole of a musical peece, Handle's Honolulu Corus.

Dec. 24: Famly party. Yung neece teeches me hustling. It's jist like a fox trottin with shoelaces tied together.

Dec. 25: The day we all wait fer and dunno what to do with till we've et, and can't do nuthin' after.

Dec. 26: Boxin Day. More blessed to give than exchange.

Dec. 27: I feel 25 pounds older.

Dec. 28: Super-bowl plugged up agin.

Dec. 29: Post Chrissmus, pre-New Yeer's party. Come home, tried to open front door with seegar butt. Wife thinks I must've smoked front door key.

Dec. 30: I'm jist gonna lie here and let my bones do ther knitting.

Dec. 31: Tonight I'm takin' nuthin' strongern musterd.

THOT FER THIS MUNTH

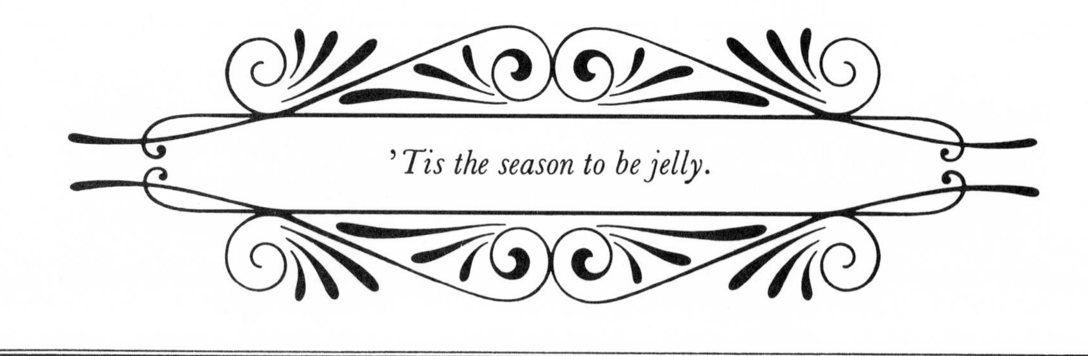

EVERYBUDDY WILL BE ON THE METRECAL

During the next decadent, every North Amerken is gonna go thru the changes. Up here in Canda we alreddy had our first flashes. Our tempacheers is now messured in Selsius, wich is yer cent-a-grade, insted of bein in Farnheet.

It takes a bit of gittin used to on an erly spring day wen the radio announcer tells you it's two above zero, and you kin see the bloomin croakacusses and you know she must be heddin fer forty. But Selsius is yer lowest common thermometer, she don't go above 100 before she's boilin at yuh.

But by gollies you keep hearing its zero, or even below zero, and sooner or later, as they keep talkin about it, she gets REELY down to blow zero, and you git a blizzard in the middle of April long after yer vermal equalnux. That's the power of suggestivness.

You see, the guvment's had no luck in bringin down wages and prices, so insted they give you cut-rate tempachers.

Now on accounta the gas shortedge, speed limits is gonna be upped th'otherway. Instedda ploddin along at fifty mile an hour, you'll be terracin' thru at a hundred kill-yer-meters. Won't be any faster, you mind, but you'll be thinkin yer gittin' more miledge fer yer money.

So soon yer gonna 'have to stop inchin yer way and lern to read yer meters. This is the kinda thing they have over in Yerp. Now you take yer Yerpeens, most of them is forners. But even the English has gone and decimated ther pound. This hole below zero stuff was invent by Dr. Selsius, a Swede. You know wat we do with Swedes round our parts? We call them rootabaggers and keep 'em cool in our root cellar, where they kin have all the blow zero they want.

YER YULE'S TIDE

Wat in the Dickens has happen to our Chrissmuss Spearits? God Help us Murry Gentile Men, has it all gone down the drane? Landlord, the Bowl is Overflowing! Is Tiny Tim becum the ghost writer in the sky? Have we reely Scrooged ourselves?

Chrismuss is sposed to be the best time of the year, fer all two-legged creechers. (Try tellin' that to a turkey and he'll tell you to git stuffed.)

Chrissmus seems to be jist shopping now, going up and down on them excavators after the boss threw you a bone-us. My boy, all he wants fer the present is a helluvacopper. Not a toy, he wants the reel thing. I'll give him the chopper all right. Give him a beenie with a perpeller on it and tell him go jump off the roof.

I dunno wat to give the wife. Last year I give her a big jar of cold cream but I had to take it back. She et more than haff the jar, and it didn't help her cold one bit.

Anyway, we'll be spending Chrismuss morning wher they spent the first one. Out in the barn. Mebbe the spearit will come back. We have the Salivation Army and the Good Will even if ther don't seem to be too much piece on erth. Speshully in yer Midleest wher the only carol they seem to sing is "No Oil! No Oil!". Seems to me yer Golden Rool has bin changed to: "Do unto Others—then cut out fast."

But, compliments of yer Festered seasoning anyway, and buy yer cards from Unisex.

BLADDER FREE NIGHTS FOR GRAVEL SUFFERERS!

"I used to arise every morning at 4 A.M. *regular as clockwork. But I was back in bed by* 4:02. *This debilitating process continued every half hour on the hour from thence as my constitution slowly dribbled away."* — N. U. Reeser. Waterdown, Ontario.

CHURCH's Red Pills for Pale People

Be cured now with a judicious use of the Kava-Kava shrub applied to the offending parts. Also affects other diseases peculiar to manhood.

"Take a stand with your kidneys"

THE CHURCH KIDNEY CURE CO. Hillsboro Tennessee.

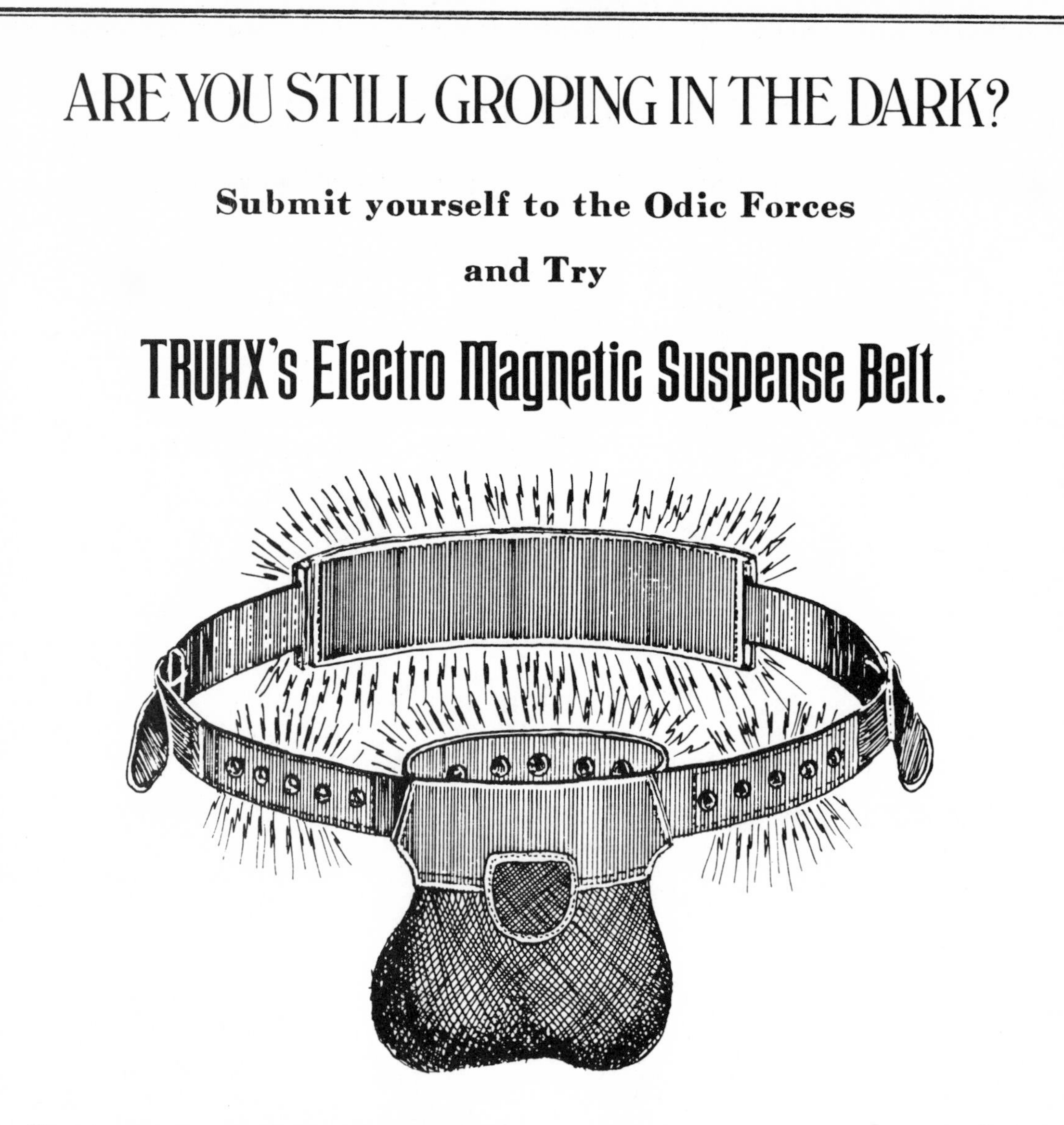

Not since Edison made the Coleman lamp icandescent has there been a force so dynamic. It cures spinal irritations, general debility, seminal weaknesses and female complaints.

"I'm thoroughly shocked but pleased." — M. M. Agincourt, Ohio.

"A lightning cure!" — W. Scott, Franklin, Penna.

"It brought back to life the most important organs of my body."
— H. L. Cooley, Tex.

"My wife took me for dead until this Vital Spark." — G. G. Revival, Kansas

"Never seen so much hell come out of one piece of twine in my life."
— J. Samples, Cumming, Ga.

A forfeit of up to five hundred dollars will be paid if a galvanometer test does not reveal a current generated by this belt.

"WE CHARGE ALL EQUALLY" **(Price on request)**

GERMAN ELECTRIC BELT CO. SPARKS STREET, OTTAWA, ONT.

Help for the Feeble in Body and Mind!!
Try this today!!! You are not wasted
WITH:
MUSTAPHA CAMEL FLUID BEEF
AND ATTAR OF ROSES
Not an injurious excitant but a Nervy renovator
Disprove your debility, and electrify your partner . . .
STRONGER THAN STRYCHNINE
MORE ARDUOUS THAN ARSENIC
FASTER THAN PHOSPHORUS. . . .
SULTANA POWER CO.
Turkey Lane, Tennessee

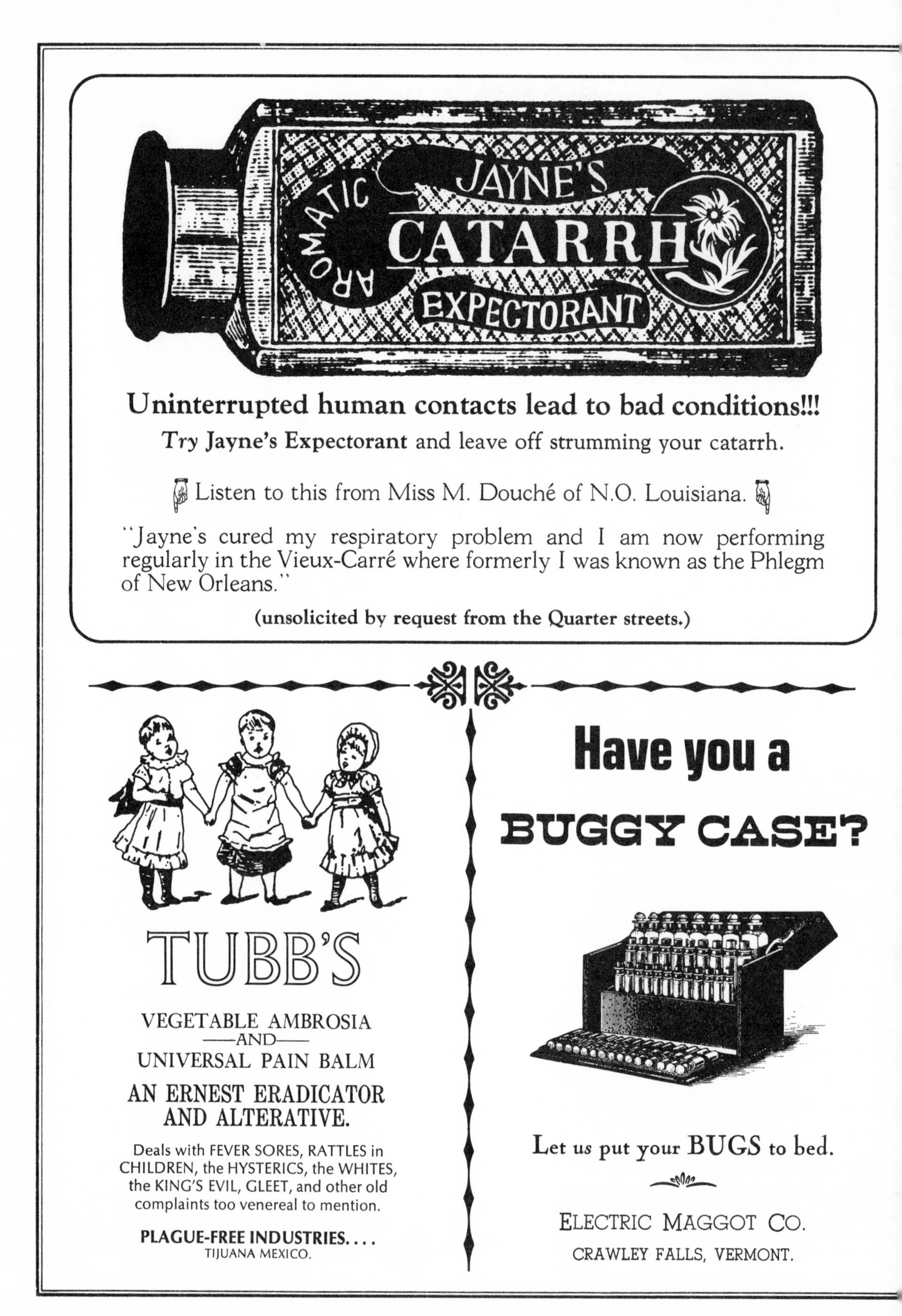
AROMATIC
JAYNE'S
CATARRH
EXPECTORANT
Uninterrupted human contacts lead to bad conditions!!!
Try Jayne's Expectorant and leave off strumming your catarrh.
Listen to this from Miss M. Douché of N.O. Louisiana.
"Jayne's cured my respiratory problem and I am now performing regularly in the Vieux-Carré where formerly I was known as the Phlegm of New Orleans."
(unsolicited by request from the Quarter streets.)
TUBB'S
VEGETABLE AMBROSIA
—AND—
UNIVERSAL PAIN BALM
AN ERNEST ERADICATOR AND ALTERATIVE.
Deals with FEVER SORES, RATTLES in CHILDREN, the HYSTERICS, the WHITES, the KING'S EVIL, GLEET, and other old complaints too venereal to mention.
PLAGUE-FREE INDUSTRIES....
TIJUANA MEXICO.
Have you a
BUGGY CASE?
Let us put your BUGS to bed.
ELECTRIC MAGGOT CO.
CRAWLEY FALLS, VERMONT.

WEATHER TO THE YEAR 2000

A Detailed Report Provided by your Fearless Civil Service
for both Canada and the United States

Probabilities to the end of the century

WEATHER: Unsettled
RAIN: Intermittent
CLOUD: Occasional
TEMPERATURES: Varying
AIR: Light, getting dark toward evening
WIND: Multi-directional
PRESSURE: Constant from high to low and back again
SEASONAL CHANGE: On and off
FORECAST BEYOND 2000: Much the same

DETAILS:

Normal temperatures will prevail. Coastal oceanic areas will be damp tending to wet. Air masses will move from west to east, bringing storms over the Rockies and drying out over the deserts, tapering off to bring eventual relief. The north will get a touch of cooler weather. Seasonable conditions will exist in the south, with not much change in variants. Fog will be patchy, tending to rain in spots, and in northern regions, the winter version of rain, snow or sleet, will make an appearance. Each Canadian is guaranteed a snow job.

Warmer weather will move in as the year progresses with a gradual reversion to cooler temperatures by the end of each twelve month span, except in the extreme south where unusual conditions will prevail as usual. Abrupt changes expected with normal seasonal progressions, and an increase of aridity where precipitation fails to materialize. In the north-west, clouds can bring a drizzling trend. Not much change in variants but warmer unseasonal temperatures bring a threat of flooding to low-lying areas. Winds will not be allowed to exceed fifty-five miles an hour on arterial roads.

Where faults exist, earth tremors are possible, but the fault is yours, not ours. The cold war and deep depressions will continue as usual.

CHIEF TUSKEGEE's DISMAL SWAMP OIL and CHILL FEVER TONIC.

As good as tobacco for ridding yourself of the plague. **Removes inivisible insects** even after you have drawn them in and they are fastened to your lungs.

☞ CLAPP AND CO. ☜

Dilworth, Minnesota

WHY PLASTER YOURSELF?

When

BEECHALAX MUSTARD LEAVES

can be

as easily carried about your person as a letter, and applied without an instant's delay.

!! TREAT YOURSELF. !!

LET OTHERS STICK IT.

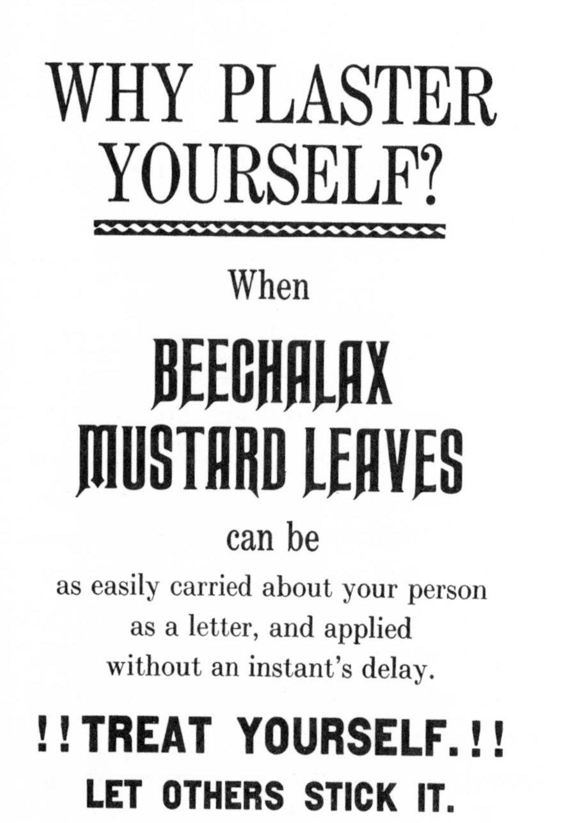

MADAME FARQUHARSON'S DREAM ALFABIT . . .

speshully for the symbol minded

What goes on wen you are asleep? Up till now, Lord only knows, but here's the cellibated mind reader, water deviner, and seer, to let you in on this under-covers operation. For all you sleepheads, here it is from A to Zzzzzzzzzzzzzzz.

AWAKE: to dream that you are awake means that you are jist not consentrating. Try closing yer eyes.

BURRIED ALIVE: dreaming that you are being inturd alive meens you are about to take a step you will soon regret. Remember there is no fewcher in any cover-up.

CARROTS: fer a young man to dream of carrots means he should take a cold shower upon arising. If the dreamer is a young woman, early marriage is advisable.

DWARF: this dream is genrally favourbull if yer dwarf is well-formed, nicely dressed and a snappy conversationalist. If on the other hand he slobbers, it means you yerself feel small and out of place, and inclined to regress things.

EXCUSE: to excuse yourself in a dream is a bad sine. Whose fault do you think it is, anyway? It's YOUR dream.

FRECKLES: to dream yer face is covert with them, meens yer chance of happyness is spotty. What did you expeck with such a rotten compleckshun?

GRIEF: to be deeply distrest to the point of tears, meens you will probly git a sociable invitation to an affair. Bring yer own towel.

HANGING: if you see someone else being hanged, there is a grate fewcher ahead of them. If it's you yerself being hung, that's lucky too. Hence the sayin . . . well-hung.

INTESTINES: to see yer own indycates something is pretty wrong. Try putting them back. If you ask frends fer assistants don't be surprised if they refuse.

JELLY: it is bad to dream of jelly in any flavor. Things are not gonna firm up the way you want.

KITTEN: if you dream of a white cat with big eyes, some woman is pulling her wool over yours. If the cat has kittens, you are gonna be surrounded by iritations. You will overcome yer troubles if you dream you drown them kittens. But let's face it, you are not a nice person.

LAKE: dreaming of this meens you are about to drain Love's cup to the last drip. But if slimy inhabitants rise up from that lake and start to chew you, this is not such a good dream. Wake up.

MANURE: overall this is a faverable omen, and good will come out of it. Jist don't spread yerself too thin.

NUTS: to dream of nuts does not mean that you are. Can be a good dream at either end, wether they appear as a appytizer or just desserts.

OINTMENT: to dream you are covered in the stuff, means that you are leaving yerself open to indiscreet advances, pervided of corse that you haven't alreddy slipped out of bed.

PETTICOAT: a bright new one, indycates you are vain. If soiled and torn, yer reputation is gittin tattered. If yer petticoat falls down at some sociable gatherin, bad luck will follow it. There is no way to win with this dream. If you realize in a dream that you have fergot to put on a petticoat at all, well, you probly never had much of a reputation to begin with.

QUILT: a good omen, provided it is placed correctly on the bed, and there is no ointment on it. I told you to stay between the sheets.

RUBBER: to dream of rubber goods shows that you are, contrary to other pinions, leeding a life of deception.

SHAMPOO: to dream you are doing this to yerself meens that yer trubbles will be soon washed away, as well as ridding yerself of a unpleasant scalp condition.

TEETH: no good ever comes of dreaming of teeth. Gums are not much better.

UNDECIDED: to dream of being undecided is a good dream. On the other hand, maybe it isn't . . . .

VULTURE: to see one of these winged murrauders of the air is a warning that somebody is about to pick on you.

WARTS: this is a "contrary" dream. As many warts as you see on yer hands, that is the number of sums of money you will receive. Mind you, wealth does not mean happyness. Besides, this dream don't always work. For example, warts fail me.

X: X-rated dreams are infreakwent, but a sine of good forchune. To dream of Xaviera Coogat x-raying his xylophone would be remarkable luck. But no one ever does.

YOUNG: to dream of being young is faverable. Unless you are young already, in which case it means nothing.

ZEBRA: You will quarl with someone close to you—probly wearing pjamas.

Reverse your Flow with

CONDY's SULPHENATED HYDROGEN FLUID (oxidized)

Drawn from medicinal springs, this floculent brownish sediment can get you on the move again. Do not be alarmed by the smell of rotting eggs. When the bottle is exposed to air, this will soon pass off. Should be drunk one hour before rising. You can give Condy to a baby!

CONDY FLUIDS • Box 8 • Tidewater, Md.

GOOD FOR MAN AND BEAST AND WOMAN TOO.

PUTNAM'S SUNDRY EMBRACATIONS

(including Ear Oil and Eye Water)

Ask for the Family Size Container to Provide a Cure for ***GARGET, WIND GALLS, SPRAINS, CRACKED HEELS, RING BONE, SPAVINS, POLL EVIL, SWEENEY, FOUNDER, LAMENESS, SAND CRACKS,*** and ***SORE TEATS*** and ***SWOLLEN BAGS.***

M. RAINES and SONS

BLACKWATER-ON-THE-GREENBANK, ONTARIO

Be Your Own GYNAECOLOGIST

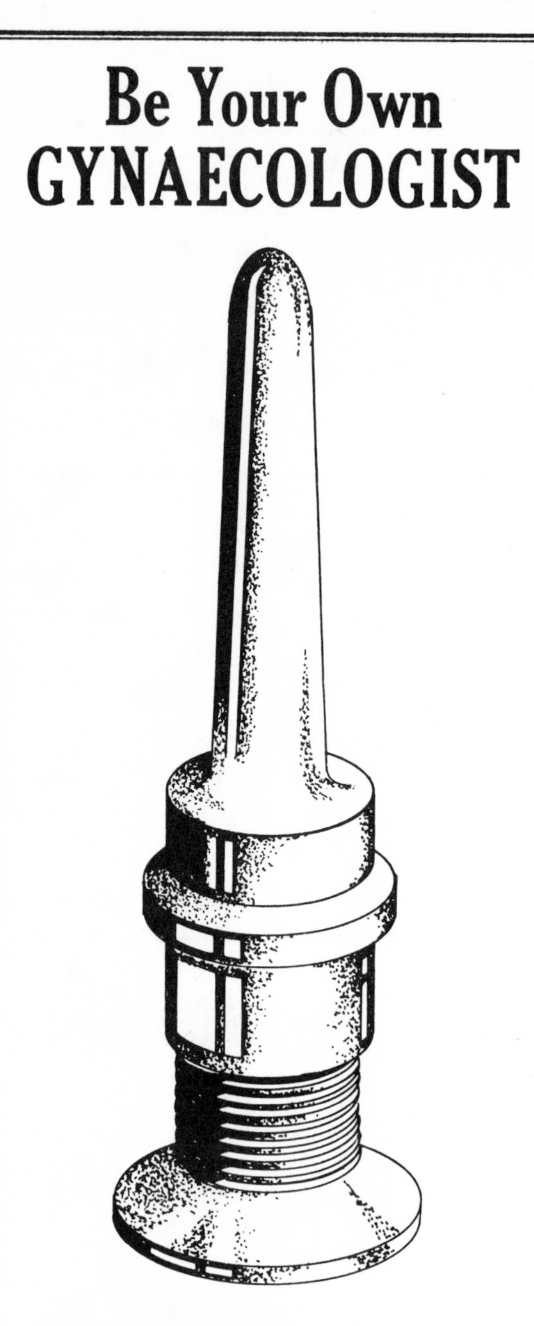

Treat yourself at home in ladylike fashion without the misery of revealing your condition to anyone. Why subject your womanly modesty to unnecessary examination by so-called medical practicioners? Avoid local manipulation and tampering.

✤ Know Thyself ✤

Do-it Urself

Box U-29
Count Luckner, Germantown Pa.

MAKE HOUSE CALLS ON YOURSELF

with

(Hard $3.95 — Soft $1.25)

Domestic and Sanitary Economy in a Hard Binder.

A new compendium for cures of all organs of the latest Period.

Including a Nursing Manual Illustrated by Hand.

Plain Directions for Prolonging Life and Descriptions of Every Part.

Home Doctor? 393 Wigmore Street, Waltham Mass.

??????ARE YOU AT PEACE IN THE GREAT CAVITY OF THE ABDOMEN??????

ARE MATERIALS BEING DISPOSED OF TO YOUR SATISFACTION?? OR IS THE COSTIVE LIVING GETTING YOU DOWN??

Try **KICKYPOO.....**

The Indian Vegetable

Family Instructor and Waist Strainer

KICKYPOO Enterprizes
Broad St. Manhattan Island